COLLECTOR'S GUIDE TO TOYS, GAMES AND PUZZLES

Wallace-Homestead Collector's Guide™ Series

Harry L. Rinker, Series Editor

Collector's Guide to American Toy Trains, by Al and Susan Bagdade
Collector's Guide to Autographs, by Helen Sanders, George Sanders, and Ralph Roberts
Collector's Guide to Baseball Cards, by Troy Kirk
Collector's Guide to Comic Books, by John Hegenberger
Collector's Guide to Early Photographs, by O. Henry Mace
Collector's Guide to Quilts, by Suzy McLennan Anderson
Collector's Guide to Toys, Games, and Puzzles, by Harry L. Rinker
Collector's Guide to Treasures from the Silver Screen, by John Hegenberger
Collector's Guide to Victoriana, by O. Henry Mace

COLLECTOR'S GUIDE TO TOYS, GAMES AND PUZZLES

HARRY L. RINKER

Wallace-Homestead Collector's Guide™ Series

Wallace-Homestead Book Company
Radnor, Pennsylvania

Published in Radnor, Pennsylvania 19089, by Wallace-Homestead,
a division of Chilton Book Company

Designed by Anthony Jacobson
Manufactured in the United States of America

Library of Congress Cataloging in Publication Data
Rinker, Harry L.
Collector's guide to toys, games, and puzzles/Harry L. Rinker.
p. cm.—(Wallace-Homestead collector's guide series)
Includes index.
ISBN 0-87069-572-X
1. Toys—United States—Catalogs. 2. Toys—Collectors and collecting—United States—Catalogs. 3. Games—United States—Catalogs. 4. Games—Collectors and collecting—United States—Catalogs. 5. Puzzles—United States—Catalogs. 6. Puzzles—Collectors and collecting—United States—Catalogs. I. Title. II. Series.
NK9509.65.R56 1991
688.7′2′075—dc20
90-70548
CIP

1 2 3 4 5 6 7 8 9 0 0 9 8 7 6 5 4 3 2 1

To
WILLIAM BOYD
He breathed life into
a fictional character
and my childhood.
I hope I never stop
thanking him.

and

EDNA JONES
Managing Editor
Chilton Book Company
After seeing the expression on her face
while reading the initial outline for this book,
I threw it in the trash
and wrote this book instead.
She was right;
I was wrong.

Contents

Preface

I hate being an adult. The responsibilities, work pressures, and societal obligations are a pain. Raised in a WASP community of strong Germanic background, I am disciple and victim of a Protestant work ethic that dominates my life. If the world were ideal, I would work and think about nothing but antiques and collectibles from the time I get up in the morning to the time I go to bed at night. Sound like anyone that you know?

Unlike most adults who can vacation to relax, I travel for relaxation only if antiques and collectibles are heavily involved. I took a cruise once. Imagine, trapped in a floating tin box for days with no "fix" available! The only thing to do was eat. By the third formal evening, I could not get my pants closed. Never again.

How do I relax? Simple. I collect toys, games, and puzzles. They keep me sane. They put everything into perspective. When I am dealing with collectibles, work and relaxation merge into one.

I am driven by one basic desire. I never want to grow up. I love the kid within me and want to see him surface as often as possible. I suspect this is true for most adults. I am just more willing to admit and do something about it than most.

What I love is the unbounded excitement that comes from acquiring a new toy, the sense of adventure from learning how it works, the pride of ownership that often borders on the possessive, and the joy from playing with it over and over and over again. Who needs drugs when there are toys, games, and puzzles?

The limitless variety of toys means that I can find one to fit my every mood. When I want to spend a few quiet minutes alone, I work a puzzle. When friends visit, out come the board games. The arrival of a specialized collector usually results in a search through my hoard for secondary items relating to their collecting specialty. When I am depressed, I favor action toys.

There was a dark period of my life when my childhood toys were placed in storage and I traveled the traditional adult course. I was on a career track that allowed no time for such trifles. Fortunately, I rediscovered Hopalong Cassidy.

In the early 1970s, while rummaging through some boxes following a move to York, Pennsylvania, I came across a cigar box filled with bubble gum cards—*my* Hopalong Cassidy bubble gum cards! The following weekend, I attended a flea market and bought a Hoppy wristwatch. Within a month, my Hoppy collection numbered over a dozen items. I had rediscovered my childhood hero—and my childhood.

While the rediscovery of Hoppy would probably have been enough, I received encouragement in my newfound madness from Ted Hake, King of Collectibles. Ted's collectibles mail auction was still in its infancy. The arrival of each catalog widened my toy, game, and puzzle horizon. I was hooked. I wanted to own it all.

At the time I was executive director of the Historical Society of York County. A principal part of my responsibility was to acquire material for public viewing. Collecting privately raised important ethical questions, so I solved the problem. I left the museum profession, my first wife, and York, winding up back "home" in Pennsylvania's Lehigh Valley.

The rest of the story is familiar to most. I began editing *Warman's Antiques and Their Prices*, created *Warman's Americana & Collectibles*, and launched "Rinker on Collectibles." Today, I am an addicted collector. I outgrew my home, my office-cabin-in-the-woods, and am located in a former elementary school, over a third of which is filled with my toy, game, and puzzle collections.

I plan never to stop collecting or playing with my toys, games, and puzzles. It is the life force that makes everything else I have to do palatable. The day my work demands allow no time for play is the day that I quit working. I know what works for me. You have to discover what works best for you. May your toy, game, and puzzle pile someday be as big as mine. But (grant me forgiveness) I wish this to happen only long after my death. He who owns the biggest pile when he dies wins.

Acknowledgments

I want to thank the auctioneers, collectors, dealers, editors, investors, writers, and others within the toy, game, and puzzle community who have taken the time to share their collections and thoughts with me. The list is so numerous that I am likely to overlook several if I try to list everyone. Rather than offend, I offer my heartfelt appreciation to all.

My staff has supported this project in a myriad of ways—conducting research, locating required books, proofreading manuscript, and seeing that I had the time to get the job done. They also appear indirectly in the text for they are also collectors. Some of the experiences cited are theirs.

The photographs came from a wide variety of sources. Special thanks to Brimfield Associates, Inc., Christie's, Christie's East, Mint & Boxed, Sotheby's, Dale Kelley of *Antique Toy World*, Bill Lango of *Toy Soldier Review Magazine*, and Wallace-Homestead Book Company's photo archive. Thanks also to the collectors and dealers who allowed me to photograph items in their collections.

Finally, thanks to all you savers around the world. Without you, our past would be lost and this book probably never written.

Introduction

I love playing with toys, games, and puzzles. I suspect you do as well. However, I am willing to bet that you rarely do. Why? Of what are you afraid? Toys, games, and puzzles are for everyone. It is time to dispel the myth that toys are only for children.

Adults unite! Join the crusade. We deserve the right to play with toys, games, and puzzles just as much—perhaps even more—than children. Our Christmas gifts and birthday presents should not be limited to clothing, appliances, and mundane utilitarian objects. Demand toys. Do not suppress the child within. Let it surface.

Insist on children's toys, games, and puzzles. For years we have been victimized by a toy industry designing and selling "adult" toys. On the surface, they appear similar to objects made for children, but the amount of time and mental energy required to play with them places them squarely in the adult realm. Adventure games are a good example. When mental strain replaces fun, reject the toy.

Once you have decided to rediscover the fun of playing, begin by raiding your own children's toy box and rummaging through the attic and basement for your childhood treasures. The nostalgia associated with these finds should be more than enough to get you hooked. As you interact with your newly discovered hoard, you are going to discover that some of your favorite toys have either been thrown out or badly damaged from use. In an effort to replace them, you'll begin attending antiques and collectibles auctions, flea markets, malls, shops, and shows. In your search, you'll notice other toys, games, and puzzles you wish you owned as a child but did not. Since you can now afford them, you start buying them. Congratulations! You have become a collector.

Buying back your childhood is not going to be cheap. You have two choices—whip out your wallet and spend, spend, spend, or take the time to understand the toy, game, and puzzle market and make this understanding work to your advantage. It is for those who see the merit in the latter approach that *Collector's Guide to Toys, Games, and Puzzles* was written.

Treat Collecting as a Game

Approach collecting toys, games, and puzzles as a game. There are rules to follow; skills achieved through dedication, hard work, and repetition. Competition is keen. Just like a game, the goal is to win. Winning is achieved when you acquire great items at great prices. Victory is playing with your purchases.

The Introduction and Part I will introduce you to the game rules for collecting toys, games, and puzzles. Reading and thinking about them is time consuming. Take the time. The better you understand the rules, the better you will be at playing the game and winning.

Unlike the rules for a board or sports game, the rules involved in the collecting game are not absolute. They are subject to broad interpretation. This *Collector's Guide to Toys, Games, and Puzzles* is my definition of the rules. Test them. Use the rules that work. Add refinements as you discover them. Reject what does not apply to your particular case. However, review the rules that you rejected once each year to see if your collecting experiences have created a new understanding of their principles.

The key to becoming a skilled collector is to collect actively over an extended period of time. Collecting skills are cumulative—the more you collect, the more likely you are to become skilled. The most experienced collectors are the ones who understand that skill building never ends. Skilled collectors are highly competitive. An antiques and collectibles axiom is: "There are no friends at an auction." It could easily be expanded to flea markets, malls, shops, and shows. The uninitiated might assume this means that all collectors are enemies. Nothing could be further from the truth. When the auction, flea market, etc., has ended, bitter collecting rivals get together to swap "war" stories and enjoy the friendship and common interests that have bonded collectors for centuries. This is what collecting is really all about: competitive friends.

I have used a competitive, aggressive vocabulary in Part I of this book. I am a Type-A personality; I like to win. I want *you* to be a winner, too. I know of no other collecting field as aggressive as toys, games, and puzzles. If you are not the competitive type, perhaps you want to consider another collecting area.

The treasures that you collect are your trophies. Do not be embarrassed to show them off. Each will have one or more stories associated with it. While they may bore your spouse and friends, these stories always find a ready audience among other collectors. If you have collected well, rivals will praise and covet. This is another of the joys of collecting.

However, the real joy comes when playing with them. As an adult who realizes their monetary value, you are likely to be a bit more careful than a child. But, never forget to play. The fun of owning toys, games, and puzzles is not seeing them sitting on a shelf, but holding them in your hands.

Before exploring the rules of collecting, it is necessary to define our terms, talk about the types of items collected, temper the "nostalgia" drive, and examine the many roles that toys play in individual lives. This is part of the hardening process I talked about earlier. Patience.

Defining Terms

Want to become confused? Look up the definitions for *toy, game,* and *puzzle* in any dictionary. *Webster's Ninth New Collegiate Dictionary* defines a toy as "something for a child to play with." *Webster's New World Dictionary of the American Language, 2nd College Edition* is a bit more generous: "Any article to play with, esp. a plaything for children." Let your imagination run wild. Think of all the things with which your children played, from the kitchen silverware to your discarded clothing. No one in his right mind identifies these as "toys." The dictionary definitions are too broad.

Note that I use "play," not "collect," in discussing toys. I neither understand nor sympathize with the collector who owns toys with which he does not play. No toy was ever meant to be worshipped; all are meant to be played with. Not to do so is a sacrilege.

There is nothing abnormal about a group of grown men pushing a Hubley motorcycle toy around a tabletop or floor. They are doing scientific research. They want to investigate how the toy works. Do not hesitate to do some investigating yourself. Who said scientific research isn't fun?

For the purposes of this book, *toy* will have two definitions. The first is "an object that was manufactured for the principal purpose of play." This is the broad, general definition, and it includes games and puzzles. The second is "a plaything without set rules or solutions." This definition excludes games because they have rules, and puzzles because they have solutions. It is the collectors' definition of toy.

Dictionaries are a bit clearer regarding the word *game*. The definition closest to the collector's concept of a game in *Webster's New World Dictionary of the American Language, 2nd College Edition* is "any specific amusement or sport involving physical or mental competition under specific rules." *Webster's Ninth New Collegiate Dictionary* uses "a physical or mental competition conducted according to rules, with participants in direct opposition to each other." The one unifying principal seems to be the concept of specific rules. In this book, a game is something manufactured for the purpose of play that has a specific set of rules. It does not take a genius to figure out that this is the definition of a toy, with a qualification.

Defining *puzzle* can be achieved in the same fashion. A puzzle is something manufactured for the purpose of play that requires a solution. A puzzle tests the ingenuity, cleverness, and skill or dexterity of the user. Difficulty is implied, but degree is open to interpretation.

All this is academic. You know how to differentiate among toys, games, and puzzles from personal experience. When in doubt, trust your instincts. You will be right 99.9 percent of the time.

Recapturing Your Youth

Although this book will discuss toys designed specifically for adults, the vast majority of the observations made will be about childhood toys. Childhood and toys are synonymous; it is impossible to grow up without playing with toys. It is the natural order of things.

Human nature dictates that all toys are not created equal in our eyes. We have favorites, the memories of which become romanticized as the years separating us from our childhood treasures go by. The model kits that I assembled in my youth were museum quality. The plastic soldiers, abused in numerous dirt piles and slag dumps near my home in Hellertown, Pennsylvania, contained such detail that they were actually real.

Rarely were our toys just inanimate objects. We personalized them. They became extensions of ourselves. They were part of the family. This is why we remember them so fondly.

What is the earliest toy that you remember? Please understand the question. You are not being asked what is the earliest toy that you have from your childhood. You are being asked to recall the first toy with which you remember playing. (No prompting from the parents in the audience.)

Parents are funny. They save our baby things. When we have children of our own, they resurrect these gems, present them to us with great ceremony, and expect us to become blurry eyed as a wave of emotion sweeps over us. I have my cast iron elephant bank, and another windup musical bank that played "Four and Twenty Blackbirds" as pictures portraying that nursery rhyme rotated through an opening in the front. Can I help it if my parents stressed saving? They lived through the Depression. I know the banks are mine because my parents told me. Do I remember them? Absolutely not!

My earliest toy memory, a wooden toy rifle, dates to my fourth year. However, the toys that I identify with my youth are those with which I played between the ages of 6 and 16. I am not alone. This is an important point. Toy collectors focus primarily on toys designed for children between the ages of 6 and 16. These are the toys that they buy as adults, attempting to recreate and recapture their youth.

There are collectors of infant's toys. A major

market development in the 1980s was the identification of Fisher Price toys as viable collectibles. Can Playskool and Creative Playthings be far behind? However, the Fisher Price phenomenon is atypical. Infant toys are not part of the mainstream of toy collecting. They are conspicuous by their absence at toy shows.

The vast majority of toy collectors are driven by nostalgia. They buy back their youth. I remember as though it were yesterday (actually, it was 1973) when I rediscovered the cigar box full of Hopalong Cassidy bubble gum cards that I had saved from my youth. At a flea market the following weekend, I saw a Hoppy watch, just like the one that I had. I bought it instinctively. Next came a Hoppy dinner plate. Before I knew what had happened, I owned a major collection of Hopalong Cassidy memorabilia.

This urge to recapture one's youth has important ramifications for toy collecting. It ensures the continual entry into the toy market of new material and new collectors. This is the principal reason the toy market enjoys a vitality not found among other antiques and collectibles.

Visit a toy store. The key to toy collecting is the bonding process that takes place between the child and his toys. I question how many children can relate in this fashion to an electronic computer game. It is not without significance that the collectibility of Atari and similar games is almost nil in today's toy market. While I have no doubt about the long-term viability of Teenage Mutant Ninja Turtle material, I do not see the variety of products that captivated the youth of the 1950s and 1960s.

Fig. 1 Childhood heroes often become the nucleus around which a toy collection evolves.

The strong reliance on nostalgia to drive the market forces us to recognize that, as the generations who actually played with certain toys die off, a new collecting rationale must be developed for these toys to hold their value. Unfortunately, the usual approach is to view these toys as "objets d'art." Values become skewed; snobbery results.

Most collectors get bit by the toy bug in their 30s. This is an ideal age. The toys from one's youth are still affordable. Collectors who wait until their 40s can still assemble the toys of their youth, but it becomes an expensive proposition. If they wait until they are 50, they probably cannot afford their toys unless they are rich.

One of the most disturbing trends in the toy market of the 1990s is the emphasis being placed on toys less than 30 years old. The Fort Apache set that I bought Harry Junior in the early 1970s now has a book value of more than $100. Harry Junior is only in his early 20s. The traditional time frame that saw an object change from second-hand junk to collectible over a 30-year span is changing.

There are several reasons for this. America has become collectible-conscious. There is a broad-based understanding among the general population that almost anything in the toy category has long-term potential resale value. The public and trade media thrive on stories of toys that are less than 10 years old being sold for five to 50 times their initial purchase price. It happens occasionally. Unfortunately, the belief is that the occurrence is typical.

As a result, more and more collectors are buying new toys as speculative investments. Rarely do they have the patience to wait 30 years for a return. Their normal holding pattern is five to 10 years. Such an approach is fine if the number of speculators remains small. This is not the case today. There are thousands speculating. The toy market will likely be flooded with 1980s and 1990s toys in the first decade of the 21st century. If that happens, the current speculative bubble will burst.

The Role of Toys

Toys play many roles: expanding one's imagination, understanding the simple pleasures of fun, enhancing deductive powers, and teaching the joy of victory and the agony of defeat. It is not uncommon to find toys that fulfill more than one of these roles. However, the toys focused on the first two roles are most fondly remembered and, hence, most eagerly sought by collectors.

The best toys allow us to imagine. Some toys point us in the direction of adulthood, such as doctor and nurse kits and happy homemaker kitchen sets. Boo, hiss to these! We grow up fast enough. Who needs toys that hasten the process? Today's children are under enormous pressure to achieve and develop. Long live childhood—it should be lengthened, not shortened. Toys are an avenue of escape from an adult world gone mad, especially toys that transport children to a land of make-believe where heros and heroines reside in abundance. Maybe this explains why so many adults collect children's toys.

Toys trigger a child's thought process. They are windows of opportunity to let the child's imagination run wild. Is He-Man from Masters of the Universe any less a fantasy than Ivanhoe or Robin Hood? Toys allow us all to live impossible dreams. The more a toy achieves this end, the more likely it is to be valued in the future.

Do not discount the "fun factor." I am talking about toys that allow us to giggle and make fools of ourselves, not simply provide amusement and enjoyment. If there is ever a Toy Hall of Fame, my nomination for the first entry is Silly Putty. Unfortunately, a sadly neglected collecting category is toys that make us laugh. I know of no collections. For whatever reasons—perhaps out of embarrassment—we devalue them.

The joy of victory and the agony of defeat are

Fig. 2 Board games should teach children to be good losers as well as winners.

most often associated with the sports world. It is a vital part of the toy world as well. In games such as cops and robbers or in a tour around the Monopoly board, someone always wins and someone always loses. Loss does not always occur as graciously as in the sports arena; therefore, it is not surprising that collectors often focus on collecting toys whose rules and skills they mastered. You can bet there will never be a Go to the Head of the Class game in my collection.

Some individuals argue that toys convey an extremely simplistic view of life. They tend to present problems that can easily be solved. What is wrong with that? The role of toys is to introduce us to the powers of deduction. In order to solve complex problems, you must first solve simple ones. Collectors favor toys that pose problems. However, I cannot understand why someone would want to own the world's toughest jigsaw puzzle. Since the enjoyment that I receive from puzzles comes from seeing them completed, I want puzzles that I can do in a reasonable amount of time. Is anything to be gained from owning a toy that confounds and frustrates? Only if you are a masochist.

Toys allow us to test limits of endurance, another important power of deduction. Alas, this often occurs to the detriment of the toy itself. As a youngster, I delighted in shoving metal cars off the end of the table to see how far they would go. It came as no surprise to me when Harry Junior did the same thing with his Matchbox cars. One knew he had exceeded the limits when the toy was damaged or destroyed. Legendary survivors have strong appeal to collectors.

Toys help us choose which individuals we want as friends. Toy owners come in a variety of styles:

Destroyers: Individuals who delight in seeing how fast they can destroy a toy. They rarely care if it is your toy or their toy. They are at the cutting edge of toy endurance testing.

Players: Individuals who enjoy playing with their toys. They are careful, but do not go to extremes. Their toys have a well-handled, well-loved, worn look about them.

Preservers: Individuals who never put their toys at risk, keep them in their original boxes, carefully check to make certain every piece or part is present before putting them away, and neatly stack them on the shelf or in the toy box at the same location each and every time. (They also neatly fold and line up their underwear in their dresser drawers.)

Sharers: Individuals who believe in the philosophy, ''my toys are your toys and your toys are my toys.'' Since they often interact with several other individuals, in a short time it is impossible to know who really owns what. Not surprisingly, most of the toys are located at the sharer's house.

Trenders: Individuals who own the ''hottest'' toy. They value toys not for their ''playability,'' but for the prestige of ownership. The minute the craze is over, they are into something else. If you are a collector, this is a personality worth identifying. Since a trender's attention span is short, his toys usually don't show heavy use; because he has little attachment to them, he abandons them when leaving home. Eventually, parents simply want to get rid of them. Toys coming from this source are usually purchased cheaply and in great shape.

As a child, I was suspicious of ''educational'' toys. They were something with which my parents felt I should play, not something with which I wanted to play. Surprise, surprise—when I became a parent, I bought educational toys for my children. They played with theirs about as much as I did with mine.

The earliest games and puzzles were primarily educational. They were also rather dull, both in appearance and playing requirements. Collectors value them for their age. Although educational emphasis faded in the last quarter of the 19th century, it never fully disappeared. It requires a special collector, one impervious to scorn and ridicule, to focus on educational toys, games, and puzzles. Fortunately, there are a few.

What This Book Is All About

Prior to the Wallace-Homestead Collector's Guide series, new collectors and dealers entering a field learned through the school of hard knocks. There is no question in the antiques and collectibles field that knowledge is both power and money. Old-time collectors and dealers jealously guard what they know on the assumption that it gives them a much-needed competitive edge.

Wallace-Homestead does not accept this archaic view, instead believing that the most valuable commodities in today's antiques and collectibles market are educated sellers and buyers. The Collector's Guides were developed to speed up the educational process. The series hallmark, "Five years' worth of knowledge in five hours' worth of reading," was not arrived at lightly.

The first part of this book explores important factors in understanding the world of toys, games, and puzzles. These include hints on collecting, building a basic reference library, pricing keys, buying and selling, surviving in a market filled with reproductions, copycats, and fakes, and cataloging, storing, and displaying objects. You should reread these chapters at least once a year. They are designed not only to provide basic understanding, but also to hone your skills.

Part I also contains two chapters of vital importance in today's market. The chapter on the international toy market is your introduction to what is probably the most significant development for the 1990s. It is followed by a report on the state of the market, providing critical analysis of the changes in the market during the 1980s and exploring the trends of the early 1990s.

Part II explores the nuances of the many subdivisions within toys, games, and puzzles. In addition to the basics, you will be shown how to learn more about each specific topic. Since collecting every known toy, game, and puzzle is outside the means and capability of any collector, this part will help you identify which categories hold the most interest for you.

There are two toy-related subjects that are not covered in this book: toy trains and dolls, each an established field with a wealth of literature. Susan and Al Bagdade's *Collector's Guide to American Toy Trains* and Dallas Mallerich's *Greenberg's American Toy Trains, 1900–1990 with Current Values* (available from Wallace-Homestead) together represent a powerful start to collecting and dealing in this area.

The Collector's Guide series will eventually contain a guide to dolls. In the interim, consult Jan Foulke's *9th Blue Book Dolls and Values*, published by Hobby House Press; Julie Collier's *The Official Identification and Price Guide to Antique & Modern Dolls, 4th Edition*, published by the House of Collectibles; or R. Lane Herron's *Herron's Price Guide to Dolls,* published by Wallace-Homestead Book Company.

Return to Those Thrilling Days of Yesteryear

Sit back, prop up your feet, and get ready to become a kid again. It is only fair to warn you that collecting toys, games, and puzzles is addictive. Once you rediscover how much fun it is to play with toys, you will be hooked. You will never rid it from your blood a second time.

PART I

BUILDING YOUR KNOWLEDGE AND COLLECTING SKILLS

CHAPTER 1

General Considerations of Collecting

This chapter is intended to destroy your neutrality. If you want to be a successful toy, game, and puzzle collector, you must continually question, analyze, and understand the *whats* and *whys* of what you see. If you do, your collection will prosper. If you do not, you will be just another collector.

Some of the discussion that ensues will make sense immediately. Other statements demand thoughtful consideration. You are not required, or expected, to agree with everything. This chapter is filled with opinions. In the antiques and collectibles trade there are no truths, only opinions. Hang on to your hats!

Mass Production

Collectors and dealers often become so enamored with an individual object that they forget to ask the critical question: *How many were manufactured?* Common sense tells us that all the toys, games, and puzzles that we cherish were mass-produced, yet we continue to ignore this critical fact.

Mass production means huge quantities. The minimum quantity is thousands. In many cases, tens and hundreds of thousands were made. Every collector and dealer should tour a toy, game, and puzzle manufacturing plant in order to understand the enormous costs involved in design and manufacturing. No manufacturer can recover startup costs with a few hundred items. Quite honestly, manufacturers experience major problems if production is less than 10,000 units.

Even objects that appear to be handmade are often the product of mass production. Americans have created the myth of the individual craftsperson carefully and skillfully manufacturing each object, one piece at a time. In reality, most make a pattern prototype that they copy over and over again. The assembly line may only produce 10 to 25 examples at a time, but it is an assembly line nonetheless.

Nowhere is this concept more evident than the wooden jigsaw puzzle. It is easy to argue that each is unique. Each was individually cut; no two are alike. If you have one that is missing a few pieces and find another identical in size and picture by the same manufacturer, you will not be able to switch pieces. Argument proven; case closed.

Not quite! At the peak of the 1908–1909 jigsaw puzzle craze, Parker Brothers employed 225 women to cut jigsaw puzzles. Each may have been working independently, but they were working in a factory environment. The cutting techniques they used were dictated by their employer. After assem-

Fig. 1-1 The Tuco Work Shops jigsaw puzzle assembly line at the Upson Company, Lockport, NY.

bling a number of 1920s Parker Brothers Pastime Puzzles, it quickly becomes evident that the same-shaped pieces keep appearing over and over again in exactly the same size. It does not take a genius to figure out that every cutter in the factory used common stencils.

Why isn't there greater mass production awareness among collectors? In large part, our ignorance is due to the manufacturers themselves. Production figures are zealously guarded. They are trade secrets. When the information is no longer of value to the manufacturer, records are destroyed and collectors are left to speculate.

For the last several years I have been researching the character Hopalong Cassidy. Hoppy was my childhood hero—I do not deny that. However, as researcher and scholar, I was most attracted to Hoppy by William Boyd's successful licensing of the character. In the 1950s Boyd blazed a trail showing the potential of commercial endorsements that remains without equal even in the 1990s. He successfully had Hoppy's or his own image displayed on thousands of products throughout the world.

As part of my research, I spent days reviewing the contracts and royalty agreements relating to Boyd's licensing and endorsements. Even I was staggered by what I found. In almost every instance, production figures exceeded my wildest dreams. No wonder so much Hoppy material survives.

In February 1950, the Milton Bradley Company of Springfield, Massachusetts, signed a license agreement with Hopalong Cassidy Enterprises to manufacture the Buckaroo game along with "Jigsaw Puzzles, Inlay Puzzles and regular children's puzzles (similar to jigsaw puzzles except that pieces do not interlock) in such design as will be approved by us, to retail at not less than 50¢ per unit." Western Printing, using the Whitman imprint, was licensed to manufacture jigsaw puzzles costing less than 50 cents. For seven years, 1950 to 1956, Milton Bradley manufactured and marketed Hopalong Cassidy games and puzzles.

The Buckaroo game became the Hopalong Cassidy game, No. 4047 in the Milton Bradley numbering system. In 1950, 173,643 games were sold, followed by 114,854 in 1951. In 1954 Milton Bradley introduced a revised version numbered 4047A. Production ended in 1956. Over a six-year span, 421,242 units were sold.

Milton Bradley issued several Hopalong Cassidy puzzle sets and frame trays. The most popular set was No. 4025, selling 379,788 units in 1950, its first year of production. In 1954 it was renumbered to No. 4025A. The set was discontinued in 1956 after selling 635,838 units in six years. The Hoppy TV puzzle, Milton Bradley No. 4143, sold a total of 60,393 units between 1951 and 1955. Hoppy Dominos, No. 4104, sold 66,724 units between 1951 and 1954. Actually, 1954 sales were only 175 units, remainders no doubt. The real life of the game was only three years.

I find that I must constantly remind myself that these are 1950s numbers and are probably typical for any popular toy, game, or puzzle of that era. Imagine what they must be for a popular toy in the 1990s. The Milton Bradley numbers are not atypical for a Hoppy license. If anything, they are low. The number of Hoppy watches produced by U.S. Time is in the millions.

Once you grasp the mass production concept and the production quantities involved with toys, games, and puzzles, you must revise your collecting perspectives. First, seriously question the

Fig. 1-2 Milton Bradley's Hopalong Cassidy puzzle set No. 4025 sold over half a million units.

terms "rare" and "scarce." In almost every case, they are meaningless. Toy dealers love to advertise a toy as "one of (blank) known." When you see this, ask yourself what happened to the thousands of others. No one really knows how many more are out there. Buying any toy, game, or puzzle on the premise that is rare is a concept fraught with danger.

Second, because toys, games, and puzzles were produced in large quantities, there is no reason to sacrifice condition when buying. Serious collectors should never purchase any toy, game, or puzzle that is in less than very good condition. The smart collector forces himself to purchase only at the fine grade and above.

Third, patience is a critical element in successful toy, game, and puzzle collecting. There is no need to snap up the first example that you see if condition and price do not meet your expectations. Shop around. Be tough. Set high standards for yourself and stick to them.

Fourth, thc quantitics of toys, gamcs, and puzzles that were manufactured mean that they enter the market from myriad directions. Successful collecting involves making your wants known over a broad spectrum of market sources. Of course, you are going to pay top dollar to top dealers for some material—it is unavoidable. But, if you do your homework, you are going to be able to purchase a surprising amount of material below book prices from many unexpected sources.

Fifth, competition among toy, game, and puzzle collectors for the top pieces is intense. The fastest way to the poorhouse is to try to buy duplicate and triplicate examples of top items to keep them out of the hands of rivals. It never works. The material was mass-produced. Sooner or later, they are going to find one. You can never own every known example. There are simply too many.

Finally, think about the relationship between the amount of goods produced and long-term value. It is a given that nostalgia motivates many collectors. Chances are that the products they remember so fondly are the ones with the highest production numbers. Yet, is it not logical that the more examples that survive, the lower the price should be? Hopalong Cassidy wristwatches, in running condition with original band but no box, sell in the $60 to $100-plus range. How can dealers justify these prices when millions were manufactured? It is extremely difficult and expensive to have the survivors repaired. U.S. Time never released spare parts to watchmakers, and Timex, the present-day version of the company, refuses to repair them. The market is bouyed solely by nostalgia. When the generation who wore the watch as children dies off, this support will be gone. Beware.

Scarcity and the perception of scarcity, no matter how false it may be, does influence price. Scarcity results from low production or an item's ephemeral quality. The key is to identify these items in each collecting category. The means is research. Since written records do not exist in most cases, the only way to determine if an item is scarce is to consult with collectors and dealers across the country over a long period of time. Unless this has been done, it is never safe to assume an object is scarce.

Collecting and Sexism

Sexual stereotypes play a major role in collecting toys, games, and puzzles. The vast majority of toy categories that are collected are those with which boys played. If you need proof, consult Richard O'Brien's *Collecting Toys: A Collector's Identification and Value Guide, No. 5* and ask yourself how many of the objects listed were designed for little girls. My guess is less than 20 percent. The situation is not quite as lopsided in the game and puzzle area.

Try as I might to suppress them, my personal prejudices influence much of what I write. I collect cowboy games, not cowgirl games. My Sun Rubber collection focuses on the company's toy vehicles, not the company's dolls. How do you explain to a female the logic behind shoving your cars off the end of a table to see how far they will fly without breaking? Ellen Schroy, a friend who is senior editor for the Warman price guides, summed it up best: "We will never see eye to eye on toys." Our sex difference makes it impossible.

Given the advances made by the feminist movement in the 1970s and 1980s, you would think things would have changed. No way! Toy collecting is a conservative bastion in the antiques and collectibles field. "Tradition" has real meaning and is respected.

In the toy category, male collectors outnumber female collectors by a ratio of 4 or 5 to 1. It is smaller in the game and puzzle category, but not by much. The American Game Collectors Association 1990 Membership Directory lists 214 members: 146 men, 59 women, and nine others (manufacturers, museums, and a few individuals whose sex was not readily apparent from their names). The ratio is close to 3 to 1. However, further analysis reveals that of the 59 women listed, 46 are joint members with their husbands or significant others. Only 13 women were listed separately.

So far, I have focused on the collector. What is the situation among dealers? I long believed that women played a more active role in toys, games, and puzzles than in the antiques and collectibles field in general. I decided to test my theory using the first 100 advertisements for dealers and auctioneers in the July 1990 (Volume 20, Number 7) issue of *Antique Toy World*. The results surprised me. Seventy-three of the advertisements were placed by men, 14 by couples (male/female), 13 by businesses that did not list the name of the

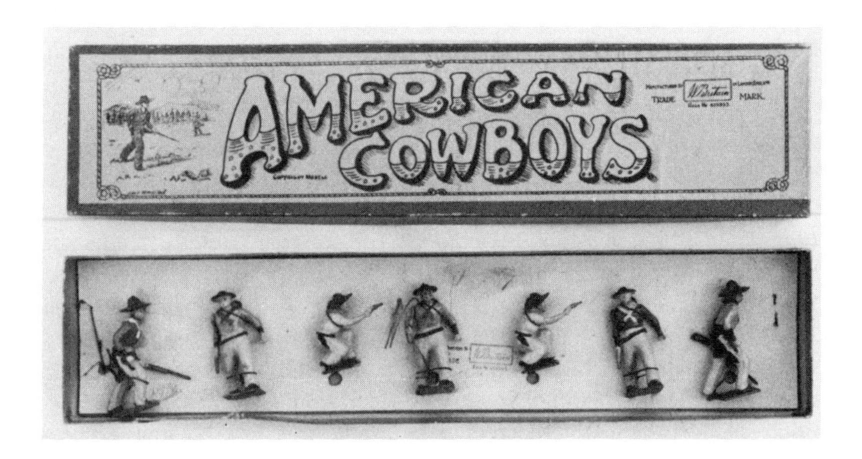

Fig. 1-3 Since people tend to collect what they played with as children, this toy would appeal mostly to males.

Fig. 1-4 This toy will be collected mostly by females.

owner, and one by a woman. Kudos to Sandra Kessler for not hesitating to challenge this male fortress.

Why did I think the role of women was greater? Clearly, the primary reason was the number of couples involved in dealing. There is a strong advantage to working the show circuit as a couple. While one person attends to the booth, the other can work the floor. For whatever reason, I encounter women in the booth more often than men.

Although I collect toys, games, and puzzles, my greatest love is puzzles, followed by games. In these two sectors women do play a more active role as dealers. In addition to the actual games and puzzles, I also concentrate on related paper ephemera (advertisements, broadsides, catalogs, etc.). Between one-quarter and one-third of paper ephemera dealers are women.

Personally, I would like to see more women collectors and dealers in the field. They are excellent scroungers and researchers. They tend to be much fussier when it comes to condition and completeness. Women are not as enamored of each toy as are their male counterparts. This is not to say that they do not love the objects—they do. But women, at least in toys, games, and puzzles, buy more with their heads than their hearts. I wish I could say the same for men, but I cannot. Women are also more moderate and flexible in their pricing.

The Importance of 1940–1945

When someone asks me what constitutes an antique, more and more my stock answer is: "Anything made before 1945." This shocks most people, which perhaps is one of the reasons I say it. However, a strong case can be made for 1940–1945 as the pivotal date differentiating antiques from collectibles.

Compare the objects that were manufactured between 1930 and 1940 with those manufactured between 1945 and 1955. There are major differences in design and theme. The American lifestyle had changed. Suburbia, television, and a new middle class produced a toy, game, and puzzle revolution.

Four things happened during World War II that set the stage for this revolution. First, many toy manufacturers abandoned toys and retooled for war production. The Sun Rubber Company made breathing masks for airplane pilots as well as rubber gaskets. Second, during the middle of the war, the use of metal and rubber for manufacturing toys was greatly restricted. Wood and paper were the dominant manufacturing products. Third, World War II scrap drives saw millions of toys sacrificed

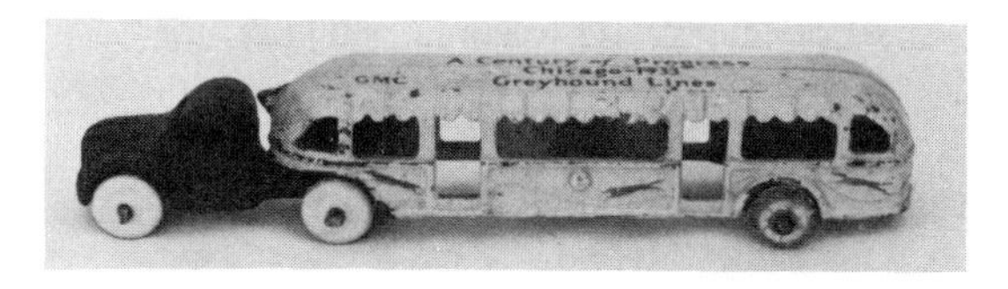

Fig. 1-5 Common style of toy before 1940.

Fig. 1-6 Typical toy of post-World War II era.

for the war effort. Finally, the war effort produced many advances in materials and manufacturing technology. Once peace was achieved, these advances were utilized in domestic production. No wonder the toy, game, and puzzle market changed.

There are other reasons for looking closely at 1940–1945. More than half of today's American population was born after 1945. If the prime motivation behind collecting toys, games, and puzzles is recapturing one's youth, the period after 1945 promises to be the most vital market place in the 1990s and into the 21st century. Even though I was born in 1941, I consider myself the product of a 1950s childhood. I am not alone.

The perceptions of collectors and dealers, whether valid or not, shape the marketplace. In toys, games, and puzzles, 1940 is the critical date. Game collectors refer to games made prior to 1940 as "antique" games. When Lee Dennis prepared the first price guide to games, the dates she covered were 1840 to 1940. She wanted nothing to do with games after that date.

Toy collectors and dealers think much the same way. The classic categories of tin, lithographed tin, and cast iron toys date primarily from before 1940. The price of toys also reflects the importance of 1940. Comparing overall category value, toys made before 1940 are priced significantly higher than toys made after 1945.

One can easily become frustrated by the fact that among toy, game, and puzzle collectors an item's age is held in far greater reverence than in many other areas of the antiques and collectibles field. Forget quality, pizzazz, and other factors that influence price. Old is often enough.

Age becomes a major problem when it is used as an excuse for poor condition. Pre-1940 toys, games, and puzzles with missing pieces and that are in fair condition and worse are held in esteem by sellers simply because they are old. Price is reduced slightly, but not by the 50 percent and more that it should be. Accept this false premise, and any collection that you assemble will be second rate.

Rinker's Thirty-Year Rule

Several years ago, I began touting Rinker's Thirty-Year Rule: **"For the first thirty years of anything's life, all its value is speculative."** I formulated Rinker's Thirty-Year Rule because I felt collectors and dealers needed a rule of thumb to deal with recently manufactured objects, especially limited edition items, that are found in the antiques and collectibles market. To assert that recently produced objects have no value would be incorrect; they do. The key question is the reliability of those values.

Why use 30 years? Basically, there are three reasons. First, time is needed for the parents of the world to throw things out. Once children get a place they can call their own, pressure builds to get their stuff out of their parents' house. Some do, most do not. Surprisingly enough, most parents have a simple solution to refusal: the trash heap. Of course, some material is destroyed through use or lost to decay. But I firmly believe the mothers of the world, more than anyone else, are responsible for scarcity in the collectible field.

Second, it takes 30 years to establish a resale track record that can be trusted. I do not care what anyone pays for something. Its value is assured only when it is resold for that amount of money or more. The 1970s and 1980s witnessed tremendous speculation in material ranging from Star Wars memorabilia to baseball cards. The problem is that enormous quantities of material were hoarded. Someday it is going to come back into the market; flooding is a major possibility.

Speculators are not willing to wait 30 years for a return on their money. They usually want to profit in five years or less. The only successful speculators are the first ones out. The rest get burned.

In the 1980s a second type of individual, the market manipulator, entered the marketplace. Individuals who, for example, successfully manipulated lunch kits from a few dollars into the hundred- and thousand-dollar stratosphere showed how easily susceptible the collecting field is to crazes. The manipulators are assisted by a strong sense of greed among many collectors and dealers. In 1991, three major collecting categories that are undergoing market manipulation are monster memorabilia from the 1960s and 1970s, cereal boxes, and plastic model kits.

Fig. 1-7 Board games from the 1950s are well within Rinker's 30-Year Rule.

Finally, it takes 30 years for individuals who have grown up with the objects to miss them, become overwhelmed with nostalgia and want to reacquire them—and be rich enough to afford to do so. Only when there is a large base of collectors can the market be tested adequately. For a stable market to exist, pieces must continue to reappear and sell for roughly the same price.

Rinker's Thirty-Year Rule should come as no surprise. Americans have a short attention span.

When was the last time you remember Americans maintaining a sustained relationship with a collecting, decorating, or fashion trend? Trends, cycles, and crazes are part of our lives. Tastes change, and prices change along with them. In the antiques and collectibles field prices can go up just as easily as they can go down. Be prepared.

Collectibles as *Objets d'Art*

A number of toys, games, and puzzles have become big-ticket items in the 1980s. Price is price. If someone is willing to pay it, it is valid. What bothers me is that many of the top prices are justified by the claim that the toy, game, or puzzle is an *objet d'art*, i.e., an object with a perceived artistic value.

Knock it off! Toys, games, and puzzles are merely toys, games, and puzzles. I do not mean to imply that they lack aesthetic quality. Many items exhibit a high aesthetic quality through their design or the image that they convey. They should be appreciated, but I am not certain they should be revered.

Two books clearly illustrate the point I am trying to make: Philip Collins' *Radios: The Golden Age* (Chronicle Books, 1987) and Scott Bruce's *The Fifties and Sixties Lunch Box* (Chronicle Books, 1988). Both were responsible for major increases in the pricing of their subject matter. It was possible to buy a Hopalong Cassidy radio in the $50 to $75 range prior to the publication of Collins' book. Bruce's efforts drove a Hopalong Cassidy lunch kit from the $25 to the $75 to $100 range.

Even worse than tagging toys, games, and puzzles with the *objet d'art* label is to apply the *folk art* and *kitsch* labels. I resent any mass-produced item being labeled folk art. Folk art is a concept promoted by dealers in order to raise prices and dupe collectors into buying a body of material, a fair amount of which is mediocre. Remember, one of the synonyms for primitive is crude. Keep that in the back of your mind.

Likewise, toys, games, and puzzles are not kitsch. They are historical artifacts that future generations will use in order to understand the period in which we live. They will prove to be far more accurate a gauge than a Knoll Robert Venturi designer chair. If toys, games, and puzzles occasionally show bad taste in design or manufacture, so what? No society is perfect. Plenty of bad taste from the past has been preserved.

It is possible to blend aesthetics, information, and fun. There is no better example than Henry I. Kurtz and Burtt R. Ehrlich's *The Art of the Toy*

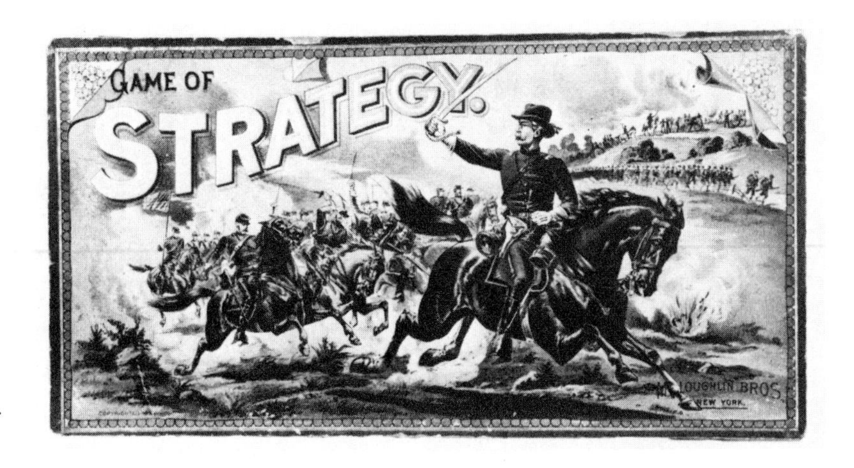

Fig. 1-8 Is this a work of art, or simply a game box cover?

Soldier (Abbeville Press, 1987). Lead soldiers have always been a favorite of mine. They are mobile, even when stationary. Your mind moves them as you look at them. Kurtz and Ehrlich have created lifelike settings for their figures. If you are going to deal with toys as *objets d'art, The Art of the Toy Soldier* is how it should be done. The book is a perfect blend of text and photographs. It is not a coffee table book, it is an adventure.

Collecting in a World Marketplace

The origin of the American toy, game, and puzzle market can be traced to Europe. The first American manufacturers merely copied foreign products. Among toy collectors, early German tin is legendary. Puzzle collectors eagerly seek early English map puzzles.

There is a strong toy collecting tradition in Europe among private individuals and museums, with several devoted exclusively to toys. Toys from the 18th and 19th centuries are preferred. Dolls and toy trains are very much part of the emphasis.

When it came to competing for European toys, American collectors were the aggressors in the past. They scoured the countryside and paid top dollar. They were the winning bidders at auction. Through the first eight decades of the 20th century, the flow of toys was from Europe to America.

This is now changing. First, European collectors and dealers have discovered the 20th century. Second, the Japanese have entered the picture. Most of the information about Japanese collectors and dealers has focused on their purchase of battery-operated and other toys that were manufactured in Japan for export in the late 1940s and early 1950s. However, they also have discovered European toys. No longer is the American toy collector the aggressor. In fact, he is in third place, behind the Japanese and European collectors.

Fig. 1-9 European collectors realize that many toys, games, and puzzles were exported to the American market.

Important to understanding this development is the recognition that much of the world was influenced by American movies, music, and television in the era following World War II. As adults worldwide start recapturing their youth, the great mother lode of material is the United States. American collectors and dealers are now facing stiff competition on the home front. As the 1990s progress, the bad news is that Americans are losing the battle. The outward flow is growing exponentially. What was good for the goose is now good for the gander.

Do Not Be Afraid to Get Personal

Chances are that the toys, games, and puzzles you collect are those with which you played as a child. There is no need to keep a stiff upper lip. Get personal. Admit you love them. Never, never apologize for doing so.

CHAPTER 2

The Right Weapon: A Collector's Start-Off Library

Once an individual is possessed by the desire to collect toys, games, and puzzles, he immediately rushes out and starts buying. Who can blame him? Isn't acquiring objects what collecting is all about? Those who counsel patience are looked upon with disfavor and disdain.

For the vast majority of collectors the joy of collecting is the hunt and kill—i.e., the purchase. Their guns are their wallets, their ammunition is colored green. No one needs a license to hunt; it is open season all year.

Novice collectors are wallet-whippers. They cannot get their wallets out fast enough. Whether it happens at flea markets, malls, shops, or shows, one is reminded of the classic western street duel. What seems to be forgotten is that someone can get hurt. Usually it is the wallet-whipper who is shot. His hasty action and lack of knowledge puts a hole in his wallet bigger than a slug from a Colt .45.

To successfully collect toys, games, and puzzles, you need the right weapon. That weapon is knowledge. Initially, you will find it on your bookshelf and in your mail box. The longer you collect, the more you are likely to replace these books and periodicals with your own knowledge. But when you start collecting, they are indispensable.

The first $300 to $500 any collector should spend should be for books, trade periodical subscriptions, and membership in collectors' clubs. Take the time to read, study, and think about the information you receive. The smart collector will devote three to six months reviewing the toys, games, and puzzles literature before buying his first object.

Just why is this so important? First, the toys, games, and puzzles field is extremely broad. You cannot collect it all. If you are going to buy to your best advantage, you must specialize from the beginning. The wallet-whippers take a shotgun approach. Buy one of these, buy one of those. The whippers build collections, but they lack a unifying theme. Reading the literature provides a sense of direction while whetting your appetite. Select the areas that interest you most. Visit toy shows and museums to check them out.

Second, trade periodicals provide useful information in two key areas: what is available and what it's worth. The faster you develop a feel for the pieces in your collecting area that are common, above average, hard-to-find, and masterpieces, the less likely you are to pay too much for them. Likewise, since prices do vary from dealer to dealer, you quickly develop an understanding of the "correct" market price for the objects that you seek. Collectors only fear paying too much, never too little.

Third, use the literature to prepare a checklist of the toys, games, and puzzles that you want to own. Most collectors collect in this fashion. Prioritize the items. Challenge yourself to add one to three objects in the hard-to-find and masterpiece class to your collection each year.

Fourth, recognize when you are developing new information on toys, games, and puzzles. Share this information with other collectors. Becoming a contributor to the toys, games, and puzzles literature is one of the fastest ways of being recognized as a valid player in the collecting community.

Finally, learn to question and be flexible. Do not assume that everything you read in the literature is accurate. If something does not make sense, either in respect to what you have in your collection or what you may uncover in the course of doing research, question it. Most authors in the field are amateurs, not professional scholars. They strive for accuracy; they do not always achieve it.

Treat all prices only as guides. Chapter Three discusses more than a dozen factors that affect price, not the least of which is you yourself. The best price guide you can find is the one that develops in your head from years of experience. When in doubt, rely on it above all others.

What follows is an annotated summary of the books, periodicals, and collectors' club publications that I feel should be in every toy, game, and puzzle collector's library. In the case of price guides and periodicals, I have ranked them in order of importance to the collector. Other listings are done alphabetically.

I have focused primarily on books currently in print. You should buy every out-of-print book that you find on your collecting specialty. These books document the evolution of the toys, games, and puzzles marketplace and are as important to your collection as the hobby horses or toy wagons themselves.

The History of Collectibles and Collectors

To be a knowledgeable player in the toys, games, and puzzles marketplace, you should have two basic pieces of information at your fingertips: an understanding of toy design and manufacturing history, and the motives and desires that drive toy collectors. Because the market is international, do not ignore toy, game, and puzzle titles printed abroad.

- Louis H. Hertz. *The Toy Collector* (Funk & Wagnalls, 1969).

A classic, Hertz's book presents the most accurate picture ever compiled of the toy market in the 1950s and early 1960s. Since this market closely mimicked the toy market of the 1920s and 1930s, in many ways the book documents a history of toy collecting in America. The chapters on starting a collection, condition and other factors affecting toy values, and identification and research are "must reads" for the modern collector. The book is long out of print. Contrast Hertz with Ruth and Larry Freeman's *Cavalcade of Toys* (Century House, 1942), a category-by-category look at toy collecting at the end of the 1930s.

- Richard O'Brien. *The Story of American Toys*. New York: Copyright by Cross River Press, Ltd.; published in the United States by Abbeville Press, Inc., 1990.

Richard O'Brien is well known for his research on the toy industry. *The Story of American Toys* is structured chronologically, using a decade-by-decade approach, starting in the 1920s. Chapters are subdivided by toy type. Unfortunately, a lack of subheads makes it difficult to determine where discussion of one type ends and another begins. Reading the book straight through is enjoyable. Trying to find a specific reference is time consuming and requires a deal of going back and forth. The index helps some.

The photographs are luxurious, an Abbeville

trademark. However, two questions must be raised by a reviewer: Are the toys pictured the most representative of each decade? And do they illustrate items readily available on the market? These matters are very much open to debate. Television-related toys are missing entirely. Character toys appear only in the early chapters. The pictures are heavily weighted to metal transportation toys and toys with a military and weaponry connotation. Although mention is made of the toys that girls played with, the book is more than 95 percent oriented to the toys played with by boys.

The greatest disappointment of *The Story of American Toys* is the lack of new information about toys and manufacturers. O'Brien has probably the finest private research library on toys in the United States. To have his book be only a "distillation of the discoveries of all of us in the field" is a grave disappointment to established collectors.

Despite its weaknesses, there are plenty of reasons to recommend the book. First, it is important to know how the public perceives the toy collecting market: *The Story of American Toys* will shape this perception. The book will attract new collectors to the toy area. What are they most likely to collect? The material that appears in O'Brien's book.

Second, if you are a new toy collector, the book broadens your horizons. You will glean information on manufacturers about whom you have never heard and learn about portions of the toy market that you have not encountered. Check the bibliography for additional pre-World War II toy book titles. The better you understand toy collecting history, the better you will be able to compete in the market.

- Harry L. Rinker. *Collector's Guide to Toys, Games and Puzzles*. Radnor, Pa: Wallace-Homestead, 1991.

What a minute! This is the book you are reading. What is it doing on this list?

It is here for one basic reason. *You need to own a copy of this book.* (It is not enough that you are reading it. You may have borrowed it from the library or from a friend; you might be browsing through it at a bookstore.) The *Collectors' Guide to Toys, Games, and Puzzles* is designed to guide you throughout your collecting career. It is a book that you should read at least once a year; each time, something in the book should cause you to reconsider your collecting philosophy and challenge your views of the field.

- Harry L. Rinker. *Rinker on Collectibles*. Radnor, Pa: Wallace-Homestead, 1989.

"Modest" is not a word that people use to describe me. "Opinionated" is. You may have noticed this from what you have already read. *Rinker on Collectibles* is a compilation of sixty columns from my weekly syndicated column of the same name. The column exists for three purposes: (1) to sing the glories of 20th-century, mass-produced collectibles (about 90 percent of all toys, games, and puzzles fit into this category); (2) to elevate collectibles to the same level of respectability as antiques; and (3) to speculate how the collectibles field functions and what motivates the collector.

It is for the third reason that you find *Rinker on Collectibles* here. The sections on market considerations, what you need to know about pricing, understanding collectors, and the future collecting market belong in the "must read" category. Contrast it, if you dare, with Elizabeth Stillinger's *The Antiquers: The lives and careers, the deals, the finds, the collections of the men and women who were responsible for the changing taste in American antiques, 1850–1930* (New York: Alfred A. Knopf: 1980).

- Blair Whitton. *Toys*. New York: Alfred A. Knopf (The Knopf Collectors' Guides to American Antiques series), 1984.

Nothing turned on the Yuppies of the mid-1980s to the antiques and collectibles market more than The Knopf Collectors' Guides to American An-

During the "golden age" of licensing in the 1950s, a single star often licensed a variety of items. One example is William Boyd, who licensed a large variety of Hopalong Cassidy toys, games, and puzzles. *Collection of Harry L. Rinker*

Evolution of the tin toy (*left to right from top*); Marx Old Jalopy (1950); Unique Art Manufacturing Company G. I. Joe and His Jouncing Jeep (late 1940s); Japanese Plymouth Fury (late 1950s); Nifty Hollywood Movie Men (1920s); and Lehmann "Also" (1917–1948). *Collection of David K. Bausch*

Cast iron transportation toys (*left to right from top*): Dent Hardware Company "Los Angeles" dirigible; Conestoga Manufacturing Company Big Bang airplane; Arcade Manufacturing Company bus; Kilgore Arctic Ice Cream truck; Arcade Manufacturing Company Model T Ford with driver; Hubley motorcycle, side car, two policemen; Dent Hardware Company tricycle; Arcade Manufacturing Company taxi with driver; and Kenton Lock Manufacturing Company wagon with horse and driver. *Collection of David K. Bausch*

NBC TELEVISION
Jan Murray's
TREASURE HUNT
$150,000
You can WIN
$25,000 CASH
WHAT WOULD YOU DO...take a mystery treasure chest with prizes from $25,000 down to a head of cabbage, or a sure

Break the Bank
An ED WOLF production
sponsored by DODGE Automobiles
Starring BERT PARKS

I'm Garry Moore . . . and
I'VE GOT A SECRET
America's No.1 TV Panel Show

TIC-TAC-DOUGH
TV Quiz Game

550 QUESTIONS AND ANSWERS
MANY POPULAR CATEGORIES
UNIQUE AUTOMATIC QUESTION SELECTOR
TELEVISION'S SENSATIONAL
THE $64,000
THE $64,000 QUE

JAN MURRAY'S
CHARGE ACCOUNT
TV word game
Play it exactly as it's played on TV

$10,000
THE $10,000 PYRAMID
GAME
AGES 10 TO ADULT
MILTON BRADLEY
BASED ON THE TV GAME SHOW
THE $10,000 PYRAMID GAME

TELEVISION'S AWARD-WINNING PANEL SHOW
WHAT'S MY LINE?
WHAT'S MY LINE?
DOG CATCHER
SYLVANIA
BEAT the CLOCK
JAN MURRAY'S CHARGE ACCOUNT

BEAT the CLOCK
BEAT the CLOCK

From the fall of 1932 through spring of 1933, several companies issued a new puzzle every week. These Depression-era "weeklies" make an excellent specialized collection. "Young Jig-Saw Makers," copyrighted © June 15, 1933, was No. 33 in Einson-Freeman's "Every Week" Jig-Saw Puzzle Series. The company copyrighted four puzzles per month from December through April, two in May, and only one in June. *Collection of Harry L. Rinker*

‹

Almost every television quiz or game show of the 1950s and 1960s licensed a game. Collectors wishing to specialize further can concentrate on shows from a single network, games associated with a particular host, or theme by which game was played. *Collection of Harry L. Rinker*

A theme collection often spans several decades. Sports games shown range from "Ya-Lo: The Football Card Game" (Ya-Lo Corporation, Columbus, Ohio; copyrighted © 1925 by E. J. Graber) to "All Star Baseball Game" (Cadaco, Inc., Chicago, Ill.; copyright © 1968). Board game collectors place a premium on box graphics but playing boards and pieces also have pizzazz value. *Collection of Harry L. Rinker*

The use of jigsaw puzzles to advertise a business or promote a product began in the last quarter of the nineteenth century and continues today. The golden age of die-cut, cardboard jigsaw puzzles was 1932—33, contemporary with the weekly puzzle craze. *Collection of Harry L. Rinker*

Kaiser Wilhelm transatlantic lines, the largest ocean liner created by Marklin, circa 1910. This first series vessel is fitted with a powerful clockwork mechanism, capable of running for 20 minutes. *Courtesy Mint & Boxed*

Metal and tin comic character toys from the 1920s and 1930s (*left to right from top*): Marx Amos 'n Andy taxi; Marx Little Orphan Annie skipping rope; unknown manufacturer Yellow Kid action toy; Marx Walking Popeye; Toonerville Trolley. *Collection of David K. Bausch*

tiques series. The pocket/purse-size format, concise introduction, analysis of each object through description, materials, marks, dimensions, maker, locality, and period, the hints for collectors, full-color photographs, evaluation clues, glossaries, and price range guides made them an instant hit. Alas, all the titles in the series are out of print, although you can find a few on remainder tables.

The chief criticism of the overall series is that it concentrated heavily on upscale material and museum examples. In the book on folk art, for example, the museum examples were one-of-a-kind objects that are never going to be available in the marketplace.

Whitton's *Toys* is traditional in approach. The majority of the toys discussed are from the pre-1930 period, so relevance to the 1990s toy market is questionable. Whitton has done an excellent job of showing both girls' and boys' playthings, thus presenting the term *toy* in a broad context. Illustrating museum examples presents little problem in the case of toys: since all but a few of the toys pictured were mass-produced, examples can be found in the marketplace. Whitton is a legendary figure in toy collecting: *Toys* is worth owning for this reason alone.

The toy, game, and puzzle markets are international. You should read a few books on world markets that do not concentrate on the United States. The following are offered as possibilities:

- Bell, R. C. *Board and Card Games from Many Civilizations*. New York: Dover Publications, Inc., 1979.

- Bekkering, Betsy and Geert. *Stukje Voor Stukje: Geshiedenis van de Legpuzzle in Nederland (Piece by Piece: A History of the Jigsaw Puzzle in the Netherlands)*. Amsterdam: Van Soeren & Co., 1988.

- Gardiner, Gordon and Alistair Morris. *The Illustrated Encyclopedia of Metal Toys*. New York: Harmony Books, 1984.

- Hannas, Linda. *The Jigsaw Puzzle Book*. London: Bellew & Higdon, 1981. Distributed in the United States by Dial Press.

- Murray, H. J. R. *History of Board Games Other than Chess*. London: Oxford University Press, 1952.

- Pressland, David. *The Art of the Tin Toy*. London: New Cavendish Books, 1976.

Price Guides

There are two key questions every collector wants to know about a specific item: (1) what is it? and (2) how much is it worth? In the 1980s answers to these questions became easier and easier to find as a wealth of general and specialized books about toys, games, and puzzles appeared. This section focuses on general price guides that cover the entire spectrum. In 1990, each category had at least one specialized guide devoted exclusively to it. This is good news for all collectors.

- Richard O'Brien. *Collecting Toys: A Collector's Identification and Value Guide, No. 5*. Florence, Al: Books Americana, 1990.

O'Brien's price guide is the toy collector's bible, widely respected and trusted. Once you have learned to use it, you will find it indispensable. The problem is learning to use it. The guide is organized by type of toy, with an occasional section devoted exclusively to one manufacturer thrown in for good measure. The approach is not alphabetical. The section on vehicles is followed by matchbox, Japanese tin, animal-drawn, mechanical banks, paper, tin windup, battery operated, soldiers, action figures, etc. You get the picture. The presentation of information within each section varies. Sometimes the principal classification is by company, other times by title, character name, or type of toy.

Scattered throughout the book are individual histories of companies, usually the first time a major listing of the company's product appears.

These histories are one of the most valuable features of the book. Many of these histories, as well as the listings and price information, are prepared by specialists who are credited at the beginning of each section, with addresses at the back of the book. Some offer collecting hints, state of the market comments, and information about reproductions. This information is a welcome bonus.

The book has no index, which is frustrating to most first-time users. Suppose you have to look up a Hopalong Cassidy, lithographed tin, windup rocking toy. Do you look under "Tin Windup Toys" or under Movies, Radio, TV"? The answer is "both." Many toys fit more than one category. When trying to locate a toy, do not give up if you cannot find it in the first place you look. Check the other sections that apply; more often than not, you'll find it.

Finally, O'Brien provides three prices for toys. The lowest price is for toys in fine condition (showing some wear in spots, but taken care of), the middle prices is for excellent condition (minor wear on edges only), and the highest price is for mint condition (like new). The principal problem is that most toys on the market fall below the fine grade. O'Brien is making the point that you should not collect toys unless they are in fine or better condition. However, this point is lost on the general user, who assumes the lowest price is for a toy that has been heavily played with.

- David Longest. *Toys: Antique & Collectible.* Paducah, Ky: Collector Books, 1990.

This guide is the new kid on the block. Comparing it to O'Brien, now in its fifth edition, would be unfair. Yet, Longest is welcome because it provides an alternate set of prices.

Like O'Brien, Longest uses a topical approach. However, this time the topics appear alphabetically. "Banks" is followed by "Battery-Operated Toys," "Boats," "Books and Paper," etc. No index is provided. Longest does include a "Games and Puzzles" category. In O'Brien, games are scattered throughout the book, and puzzles are largely neglected. Longest uses a price range. Ranges are often so broad as to be meaningless (e.g., $50 to $350 for a Marx Superman windup tank toy). Again, Longest uses a low range that represents very fine condition (no major flaws and worthy of being collected). Experienced toy collectors would argue strenuously over his definition of *very fine*. It is hard to interpret Longest's pricing meaningfully.

When comparing similar items, Longest's descriptions lack the detail and clarity of those found in O'Brien. Notably missing are dimensions and notations to indicate variation. Yet, there are hundreds of toys that appear in Longest that do not appear in O'Brien. This is the great value of having more than one general guide. There are hundreds of thousands—perhaps millions—of toys. No guide can present them all.

- Richard Friz. *The Official Identification and Price Guide to Collectible Toys, Fifth Edition.* New York: The House of Collectibles, 1990.

The fifth edition is actually Friz's second effort. He deserves credit for recognizing and correcting many of the serious flaws found in the fourth edition that he edited. Organization is topical and presented alphabetically. The book emphasizes quality of the listings rather than quantity.

Like many of The House of Collectibles publications, the book focuses on information that is readily available from auction catalogs. Distorted, rather than uniform, coverage results. For example, 53 pages of the book's 403 pages listing prices are devoted to military miniatures, 79 pages to transportation vehicles. The balance of the 24 topics fit into the remaining two-thirds of the book. (Gone entirely from the fifth edition is the "toy trains" category that took up 116 pages of the fourth edition's 432 pages of price listings—a wise choice.)

Friz alternates between fixed prices and price ranges. He does deserve a medal for keeping his price ranges meaningful. What is missing in his discussion in "The Prices in This Book" section is the condition level that is used to establish prices. Comparing Friz's prices with O'Brien and Longest, the base seems to be a toy in very good to fine condition. There is an index, thank goodness. It is not great, but it is there.

The first 90 pages of Friz's book are actually a condensed collector's guide to toys. Topics such as buying and selling at auction, housing your collection, and documenting a toy by maker and date of manufacturer are typical. His list of manufacturers (including working dates and a brief history) is most helpful, but weak in manufacturers of the post-World War II period.

No matter what their attributes or faults, you need all three of the above price guides, if for no other reason than to know what information others are using to set prices. Price guide editors may view themselves only as reporters, but the truth is that their information is used to set prices.

A second reason for owning all three is their bibliographies and lists of auctioneers, dealers, collectors' clubs, museums, publications, and restorers. You will find many specialized sources listed.

- Lee Dennis. *Warman's Antique American Games, 1840–1940*. Willow Grove, Pa: Warman Publishing Company, 1986.

Essentially a priced picture book, organized by company. Under each company, games are listed alphabetically. Detailed descriptions for each game include name, type of game, copyright date, size of box, number of pieces, detailed listing of pieces, type of instructions, and details about the game board. Additional sections of listings and prices only are provided for Milton Bradley, McLoughlin Brothers, and Parker Brothers products.

The introductory material contains information covering the history of games, how to collect games, and keys to displaying games. A game title index makes finding games included in the book easy. Only two major collections were used to prepare the book, thus explaining the weak representation of post-World War I games. The book went out of print in 1989. Damaged copies were sold to the American Game Collectors Association, which still has a few copies for sale.

On September 17, 1988, Robert W. Skinner, Inc., sold the games and puzzles of The Game Preserve Museum, the private collection of Lee and Rally Dennis of Peterborough, New Hampshire. Although most of the lots contained more than one game, enough games sold singly to provide a comparison between market reality and the prices found in the Dennis guide. In several instances, the multiple between the book price and auction price was five or greater. As a result, game prices, especially for those made prior to 1915, skyrocketed overnight.

Bruce Whitehill, a major collector and dealer in games, is currently collecting information for a combination collector's guide and price guide to games, expected to cover games from the 19th century to the present. Publication is scheduled for the early 1990s.

- Anne D. Williams. *Jigsaw Puzzles: An Illustrated History and Price Guide*. Radnor, Pa: Wallace-Homestead, 1990.

Williams' book combines a collector's guide with a priced picture guide. The first 70 pages include chapters on jigsaw puzzle history, major jigsaw puzzle manufacturers, collecting hints for developing a collection, and a discussion of the factors that influence puzzle prices. The second part presents more than 700 photographs of puzzles, organized topically. Price information appears in a guide in the back.

Because of the tremendous number of jigsaw puzzles produced, especially by the large die-cut, cardboard puzzle manufacturers, finding your exact puzzle pictured is difficult. Users must find a comparable puzzle and then raise or lower the suggested price depending on the plusses and minuses of the jigsaw puzzle they own.

There appears to be a strong feeling among collectors that Williams' book will trigger a price increase for jigsaw puzzles. Shortly after plans to publish Williams' book were announced, the June 1990 *Kovels on Antiques and Collectibles* newsletter reported: "Here's a chance to stay ahead of the market. A new book on jigsaw puzzles is slated for publication in August, and prices are likely to take a giant leap. Buy now, before word gets around." Williams had labored long and hard to make certain that the prices in her book were a true reflection of the market, but her efforts may have been undermined by seeds of doubt.

One of the most important features of Williams' book is an index of American puzzle manufacturers between 1850 and 1970 that appears in the appendix. Although not encyclopedic, the listing is the most comprehensive list of puzzle manufacturers published to date. No doubt, its publication will generate much new information that would have remained hidden were it not for this initial effort.

Jigsaw Puzzles: An Illustrated History and Price Guide covers only picture puzzles. But skill and dexterity puzzles also are part of the puzzle field. For information on these, consult Jerry Slocum and Jack Botermans' *Puzzles Old & New: How to Make and Solve Them* (University of Washington Press, 1987). Unfortunately, the book contains no information on prices.

Periodicals

The vast majority of information about toys, games, and puzzles reaches collectors through periodicals—magazines and newspapers—directed to their specific collecting interests. This is not to suggest that general periodicals, such as *Antiques & Collecting Hobbies* (1006 S. Michigan Ave., Chicago, IL 10605) or *Antique Trader Weekly* (P.O. Box 1050, Dubuque, IA 52001), do not run stories or advertisements concerning toys, games, and puzzles. It behooves the toy, game, and puzzle collector to subscribe to them as well.

How much time can one devote to periodicals and still meet the other demands of collecting? The problem facing today's collector is too much information, not too little. No collector has the time to read 10 to 15 general trade periodicals each month. More and more collectors are turning to periodicals that focus on their specific collecting needs.

The toys, games, and puzzles periodical market is currently dominated by a magazine, *Antique Toy World*, and a newspaper, *Toy Shop*, each serving two separate constituencies. They are challenged by a host of other periodicals that provide broad market coverage and attract national advertisers. On the horizon are several proposed specialized quarterlies, for example, one on games and another on action figures. The desktop publishing revolution has opened the door to this development.

What are collectors and dealers going to do? Collectors resent having to spend hundreds of dollars a year to keep their subscriptions renewed. Yet, they crave knowledge and turn to any periodical that promises to discuss their favorite toys, games, or puzzles on a regular basis. Auctioneers and dealers see their advertising dollars spread thinner and thinner. Unfortunately, the gauges to measure which advertising draws and which does not are extremely poor.

There is strength in unity. Because of the enormous diversity within the toys, games, and puzzles collecting community, there is a strong tendency to fractionalize. You must resist this. For every narrowly oriented periodical to which you subscribe, subscribe to a second that covers the general market. Follow the same practice when attending toy shows.

- *Antique Toy World*. P.O. Box 4509, Chicago, IL 60634. 1991 subscription: $25.

Antique Toy World covers the middle and high end of the market. Each issue contains three to four articles dealing with the history of toys and two to four reports on toy auctions, shows, or collectors' activities. The articles are extremely chatty in tone and often provide no documentation for the facts presented. The auction and show reports have surprising balance, discussing what did not sell along with what did. The format is primarily black and white. There is a center color insert devoted to advertising.

The publication's greatest strength is its advertisers. Every major dealer, toy auction, and toy show advertises. The reason is simple: The advertising rates for *Antique Toy World* are the lowest in the business. In pictorial advertising, approximately three-quarters of the toys are priced. This is unheard of in magazines in other collecting areas.

Because of its strong impact on high-end American toy collectors, European and Japanese dealers and collectors also advertise in *Antique Toy World*. The magazine reciprocates by reporting on foreign toy shows and including their dates in the calendar of events.

Antique Toy World is an excellent source of information on specialized collectors' clubs, toy restorers, and new publications. The classified advertising section is weak. The rates compare favorably to *Toy Shop*, but the circulation does not.

- *Toy Shop*. Krause Publications, 700 E. State St., Iola, WI 54990. 1991 subscription: $18.95.

Toy Shop is an advertiser's dream. The entire paper is devoted to classified and display advertising; there is no editorial content. The paper measures 11″ × 14 ½″, uses a four-column format, and has more than 120 pages per issue.

The paper is organized alphabetically, first by type of toy and then by manufacturer. It covers all aspects of the toys, games, and puzzles market. Its greatest strength is that the bulk of its advertisers sell middle-market and low-end material. There are plenty of items offered for sale for less than $15. The paper also carries a number of specialized features, such as announcements, collectors' club information, a business directory, and a show directory. A first class subscription rate ($38.75) is available for those subscribers who cannot wait.

Scanning the paper is rarely satisfactory; it needs to be read thoroughly. Many advertisements contain offerings from a broad range of toy, game, and puzzle categories. Pay special attention to the "Non-Toy Misc." category. Some important secondary material related to toys, games, and puzzles appears in these advertisements.

Toy Shop is just one of Krause Publications' products. Krause also publishes major weeklies or monthlies in the automotive, baseball card and memorabilia, comic book, firearms, music, numismatics, record, and sports collecting categories. They have a strong book publishing program as well. In 1990 Krause published Fred Grandinetti's *Popeye, The Collectible*. Additional toy titles are being considered.

- *Model and Toy Collector*. 330 Merriman Road, Akron, OH 44303. 1991 subscription: $15.

Model and Toy Collector, a quarterly, is published by Bill Bruegman, owner of Toy Scouts, Inc. Issues vary between 36 and 40 pages and are primarily editorial. There are one to two pages of classified advertising, a few pages of display advertising, letters to the editor, and an update section covering the latest news, books, and reproductions in the toy world.

Non-subscribers will want to acquire the special issues devoted to one single character. The Spring 1989 issue, No. 12, honored the anniversary of Batman and Robin. The Summer 1990 issue, 64 pages, focused on Dick Tracy. Back issues can be ordered by sending $5 per issue.

- *Collectors' Showcase*. P.O. Box 837, Tulsa, OK 74107. 1991 subscription: $36.

Collectors' Showcase is a lavishly illustrated full-color magazine. Although dealing with a broad spectrum of collectibles, a large number of its articles focus on toys, games, and puzzles. The editorial content of most articles is short, but there are usually more than 25 illustrations.

Each issue contains six to seven feature articles, some of which may focus on a museum or special toy anniversary. Regular department features include auction reports, book reviews, collectors' calendar, and a classified advertising section that features full-color pictures of wanted material. As in *Antique Toy World*, some advertisers price their objects.

Advertising rates for *Collectors' Showcase* are expensive compared to the other toy periodicals. As a result, primary advertisers are middle-market and high-end auctions, dealers, and shows. Because of the cost, key dealers do not always advertise in every issue. Make certain you check several issues when assembling a dealer list for your file.

Sports Magazines of America, Inc., acquired *Collectors' Showcase* in 1988. D. Keith Koanis and Donna Koanis, who founded the magazine, remained with it for approximately one year after the acquisition. Recently the Koanises have started *Inside Collector*, a *Collectors' Showcase* look-alike.

- *Toy Values Monthly*. Attic Books, Inc., 19 Danbury Road, Ridgefield, CT 06877. 1991 subscription: $24.

In late 1990, Attic Books, publisher of a monthly price guide to comic books, announced its entry into the toy world with *Toy Values Monthly*. This monthly approach puts toys on a par with baseball cards, cars, comic books, guns, postcards, sports collectibles, stamps, and records—all of which have monthly publications. Since none of the general toy price guides are revised annually (most are on a three-year cycle), *Toy Values Monthly* provides the collector with much more current pricing.

Attic Books plans to cover sixty major toy categories in a ten-month cycle. Advisors are being utilized for each category. The approach is alphabetical. The premier issued covered action figures, aircraft, banks, bicycles, books, and buttons. Limiting the number of monthly topics allows for in-depth listings. Each issue will contain a minimum of 10,000 listings.

While major shifts do occur in the toy market in the course of a year, Attic Books' format keeps these changes in perspective. Several of the monthly baseball card publications change pricing each issue, giving the feeling that the baseball card market is in a continual state of flux. This is a concept that the toy market would do well to avoid.

Toy Values Monthly is the perfect companion to *Antique Toy World* and *Toy Shop*. These are the three toy market publications to which every collector *must* subscribe.

- *Toys At Auction*, Haimowitz & Cloud, 405 Ninth Street, Brooklyn, NY 11215.

Toys are an important part of the auction scene, from back porch country sales to catalog auctions by major New York City houses. Haimowitz and Cloud, utilizing modern computer technology, plan to provide an alphabetical listing of toys sold at auction on a quarterly basis.

The first *Toys at Auction* list appeared in August 1990 and was 28 pages in length. Auction houses represented on the list included Christie's, Lloyd Ralston Auctions, Lashway's Auctions, New England Auction Gallery, Nostalgia Galleries, Richard Opfer, Saugerties Auctions, Smith House, Skinner's, and Ted Maurer. The next three quarterly issues supplement this initial listing. Each July a major new listing will be published.

The list is prepared alphabetically by toy title. Listing information, which unfortunately is minimal, relies heavily on abbreviations. The compilers make the assumption that the user has access to the catalogs from these auctions to obtain more details if required. This is not true for most collectors. They also do not adjust their final price listings by calculating the buyer's premium where applicable. Failing to do this leads to confusion.

The introduction to the listing contains the following: "*Toys At Auction* uses mainly prices realized at toy auctions, rather than general sales that may include a few toys here and there. We feel that the former will provide a more accurate view of prevailing prices.'' This is a flawed approach. Dealers purchase the vast majority of auction items. When they offer them for sale, they are priced considerably higher than they paid.

Further, *Toys At Auction* makes no attempt to list every toy sold at each auction. The approach is selective. Since the compilers are dealers, they have a vested interest in maintaining a strong price image. A compilation of toy auction prices will prove helpful. *Toys At Auction* is a start, albeit a weak one.

- *U.S. Toy Collector Magazine*. P.O. Box 4244, Missoula, MT 59806. 1991 subscription: $14.95.

Do not be deceived by its title. *U.S. Toy Collector Magazine* does not cover the entire field of toys, games, and puzzles. Its subtitle is, ''The American Journal of Vehicular and Transportation History.'' Vehicles and other transportation-related material represent such a large part of the toy market that *U.S. Toy Collector Magazine* deserves to be listed in this general section. Several of the magazine's advertisers do offer other types of material as well.

The magazine has a strong emphasis on New York/New Jersey, the Midwest, and the West Coast (especially California) in respect to its contributing writers, its advertisers, and the shows it covers. An average issue runs 80 pages, of which three-quarters is advertising. The practice of pricing material for sale is strong.

U.S. Toy Collector Magazine is oriented toward the middle market. The vast majority of advertised toys list between $25 and $400. It is also strongly pro-collector, editorializing against market dealers and manipulators who inflate prices.

- *YesterDaze Toys*. P.O. Box 57, Otisville, MI 48463. 1991 subscription: $12.

This paper began full of promise. It was an offshoot of *The Daze*, a newspaper devoted to 20th century American glass and china. What made it so special was that the staff was female and the focus was on toys with which girls played. It provided the much-needed balance to the male-dominated periodicals.

Alas, *YesterDaze Toys* publisher Terri Steele had to take over *The Daze* after the death of Nora Koch, her mother. *YesterDaze Toys* stumbles along. Issues run approximately 30 pages. The bulk is advertising, much of it filler. Rates are approximately 50 percent higher than *U.S. Toy Collector*. As this book went to press, Terri Steele affirmed her intention to keep *YesterDaze Toys* alive.

- *The Toy Collector Magazine*. P.O. Box 08350, Milwaukee, WI 53208. 1991 subscription: $23.95.

In June 1990, the premier issue of *The Toy Collector Magazine* promised to ''bring you information about the most popular toys of the day—from the early 1900s to the present. I'll tell you why toys are collectible and who collects them. If you want to begin collecting but don't know where to start, I will help you out. . . .''

It is hardly fair to judge a periodical by its first issue. The feature article was basic and contained no new information. The interview with a collector of toy soldiers was much more refreshing and informative. As one might expect from its location, dealer and show advertising was primarily Midwestern.

The Toy Collector Magazine was scheduled to begin publishing monthly in 1991. The conservatism of toy collectors and dealers makes starting any new venture a risk. If this magazine is still being published when you read this book, consider becoming a subscriber.

- *PCM* (Paper Collectors' Marketplace). P.O. Box 127, Scandinavia, WI 54977. 1991 subscription: $15.95.

Why is this periodical on the list? It is not a specialized toy, game, or puzzle publication. However, it is the leading classified advertising source for paper ephemera. A great deal of material related to toys, games, and puzzles is offered for sale in its pages.

As you collect toys, games, or puzzles, you will quickly find that the actual objects are only part of the story. Manufacturers' catalogs, advertising broadsides and displays, magazine advertising, and photographs showing children playing with your favorite toys are just a few of the items that you may want to supplement your collection. These items appear in *PCM*. In addition to making dealer contacts, *PCM* also is helpful in locating paper ephemera shows in your immediate area. Advanced toy, game, and puzzle collectors haunt these shows as regularly as they do their own specialized shows.

Gone, but Not Forgotten

Periodicals come and go. Not all survive. Yet, in the ghosts that haunt the shelves of old-time collectors is information on toys, games, and puzzles that has never been published anywhere else. Keep your eye open for these publications and acquire them whenever possible. In order of importance, they are:

- *Collectibles Illustrated*, published by Yankee Publishing between 1982 and January-February 1985. The articles were pizzazz-oriented. The famous and obscure along with their collections were featured. *Collectibles Illustrated* was slick, in full color, national in scope, and a failure. Won't someone please try again?
- *Collectibles Monthly*, published by Ted Hake between June 1977 and April-May 1979. This publication, more than any other, marked the coming of age of the 20th century collectibles market of which toys, games, and puzzles are such an important part. Collectors and dealers, including Noel Barrett, Virginia Botsford, Robert Cauler, Ken Chapman, Ted Hake, Robert Lesser, and George Theofiles, contributed articles and comments.
- *Rarities*, published by Behn-Miller Publishers in the early 1980s. It was doing well until Yankee Publishing purchased and killed it. The mailing list was used for *Collectibles Illustrated*.
- *Collector's Corner*, published by A.L. Jones in 1988. It lasted only 10 issues. Some of the articles you missed concerned blood-letting tools, calling cards, Christian medals, rubber Civil War items, Daniel Boone memorabilia, elongated coins, firehouse collectibles, harmonicas, the KEEN KUTTER company, mottos, shaving pens, swizzle sticks, Viking theme collectibles, and much, much more. Perhaps the article mentioning the Scat Museum of animal droppings may have gone a bit too far, but hey, don't you have a sense of humor? It is a classic.

Another type of ghost is back issues of still-published periodicals that you do not own. Many of these periodicals offer back copies for sale. If you can afford to acquire them, they will prove a wise investment in time. Many of the backlists indicate the articles published allowing you to be selective.

Reference Books

You cannot tell the players without a score card. How many of these cartoon, radio, and television characters would you recognize: Sgt. Bilko, Mr. Bluster, Major Bows, Buttercup, Ella Cinders, Uncle Fester, Gracie, Happy Hooligan, Humphrey, Kayo, Kuryakin, Lucky Pup, Jerry Mahoney, Mary Marvel, Fibber McGee, Red Ryder, Mortimer Snerd, Spark Plug, Captain Video, and Winnie Winkle? Less than five out of 20? Feel like a dummy?

Toy, game, and puzzle values rest in part on knowing exactly what you have. A white metal pinchusion of a round-headed boy with large ears, dressed in a flowing robe with "I'M WEIGHTIN FOR YER 'SEE'" is a $50 sewing collectible unless you identify the figure as the Yellow Kid, at which point it becomes a $200-plus item to a character toy collector. There are hundreds of thousands of cartoon, movie, radio, and television characters. You cannot expect to know them all.

You need to spend some money on reference books. A word of warning: they are not cheap. Make them an up-front investment. They will pay for themselves within your first three years of collecting by allowing you to find bargains that you otherwise would have passed.

The following reference books are a start. As you focus on one specific category of toy, game, or puzzle, you will discover others. Spend the money to buy them.

- Brooks, Tim and Earl Marsh. *The Complete Directory to Prime Time Network TV Shows, 1946-Present, Third Edition*. New York: Ballantine Books, 1985.
- Horn, Maurice (editor). *The World Encyclopedia of Cartoons*. New York: Chelsea House Publishers, 1980.
- Horn, Maurice (editor). *The World Encyclopedia of Comics*. New York: Chelsea House Publishers, 1976.
- Rovin, Jeff. *The Encyclopedia of Super Heroes*. New York: Facts on File Publications, 1985.
- Terrace, Vincent. *Encyclopedia of Television: Series, Plots and Specials—1937–1973*. New York: New York Zoetrope, 1986.
- Terrace, Vincent. *Radio's Golden Years: The Encyclopedia Of Radio Programs 1930–1960*. New York: A.S. Barnes & Company, 1981.

You can order these books through your local bookstore or through a dealer who specializes in antiques and collectibles books. The specialized dealers advertise in the trade papers. *Maine Antique Digest* and *The Antique Trader Weekly* are two good sources.

Every major toy show has one or more bookseller. These individuals sell not only books, but sample issues of periodicals as well. Blystones' (2132 Delaware Avenue, Pittsburgh, PA 15218), a mail order bookseller, specializes in books related to toys (including dolls and toy trains), games, and puzzles, and will send a list upon receipt of a self addressed, stamped envelope. In addition to booksellers, many dealers sell books and periodicals relating to their specialties.

Collectors' Clubs

- American Game Collectors Association. 4628 Barlow Dr., Bartlesville, OK 74006.

The American Game Collectors Association (AGCA) has a number of lofty goals: to uncover and share information about early games and companies, to expand the public's awareness of games, both as an art form and as a historical reflection of American culture, to establish a network of game collectors, to bring collectors into contact with others who want to buy, sell, and trade games, and to bring collectors together at a national convention held annually in the fall. AGCA provides its members with four publications: *Game Times*, *Game Researcher's Notes*, *The Game Catalog*, and a membership directory.

Games Times is the AGCA's newsletter. It contains news of AGCA events, information on auction prices, books, shows, and other events in the general collectibles field, a concise history of one or more game companies (perhaps its most valuable feature), and classified advertising. *Game Researcher's Notes* reports on individual members' research, material received by the AGCA archives, game company history, and some membership news. Because its publication alternates with *Game Times*, there is a tendency for information to overlap.

The Game Catalog is a 117-page listing of games made in America before 1950. It is organized by manufacturer and title, and is an invaluable reference tool. Debbie LaRue (5310 240th Ave. NE, Redmond, WA 98053) is spearheading the effort to prepare a similar listing for post-1950 games.

The AGCA has established an archive whose holdings are divided into: (1) instructions and rules; (2) commercially produced catalogs; (3) catalogs of AGCA members' collections; (4) auction catalogs; (5) games; (6) journals; (7) books; (8) ephemera; and (9) the official papers of AGCA. Imagine, a place where you can find the instructions for almost every game ever produced in America. There is no longer any need to turn down a game because the instructions are missing. AGCA members pay $1 per set of instructions ordered; the price to the general public is $4. Photocopies of catalogs cost members approximately $5; non-members pay double the members' cost.

The AGCA membership directory is not content with a simple listing of name, address, telephone number, and a few remarks about a member's collecting interest. The directory also includes information on members' collections, whether they sell or trade, their specific buying wants, their secondary collecting interests, and areas in which they are doing research. The directory also provides some biographical data on members and states the conditions under which they welcome other collectors.

In addition to its annual convention, AGCA is sponsoring a number of regional meetings. All meetings include visits to local members' collections, lectures, a game auction, and a game exchange (i.e., show and sale).

- Antique Toy Collectors of America. 2 Wall St., New York, NY 10005.

Membership is by invitation only. Twelve new members are admitted each year by invitation, but only when established members do not renew. You have no chance of being admitted if you are not an established collector. Your application must be supported by two members, and final acceptance depends on a vote of the full membership. Because of the relatively few vacancies, there is a waiting list. Members collect in the most traditional toy collecting categories, and most focus on pre-1940 toys.

The association meets twice a year in different locations. A newsletter is published, but is restricted to members. The association also reprints old toy catalogs, which are distributed to members. The owner of the original catalog receives 100 copies that he may distribute as he sees fit, which is how some of these catalog reprints enter the general market.

- Ephemera Society of America. P.O. Box 37, Schoharie, NY 12157.

Ephemera is the minor transient documents of everyday life—material that was destined for the waste basket but never quite made it. The term is used interchangeably with paper collectibles, but this is a very narrow view; there is plenty of ephemera made from other materials. An excellent introduction to the subject is Maurice Rickards' *Collecting Printed Ephemera* (distributed in the United States by Abbeville Press).

The two principal publications of the society are a newsletter, *Ephemera News*, and a membership directory. The newsletter is chatty, contains book notices, some classified advertising, and paper show advertising. The membership directory is excellent because it lists members' specific collecting needs. Several actively collect toys, games, and puzzles.

The society's annual meeting corresponds with a major New England paper show. It is not unusual to find a toy-related topic on the meeting program. Occasionally, the special show exhibit is related to a toy, game, or puzzle.

CHAPTER 3

Factors that Influence Price

''How much is that worth?'' is one of the most debated questions in the toys, games, and puzzles field. There is really only one answer: An item's worth is known only when a buyer and seller agree on a price and a transaction occurs. There is no fixed value for any toy, game, or puzzle.

This can be extremely frightening for someone accustomed to the practices of a department or grocery store, where prices are fixed. Prices for toys, games, and puzzles fluctuate. The same toy priced at $50 in one dealer's booth may be priced at $100 in another. So the question is, what is the *fair market value?*

The Internal Revenue Service definition begins: ''The fair market value is the price at which the property would change hands between a willing buyer and a willing seller, neither being under any compulsion to buy or sell and both having reasonable knowledge of the relevant facts.'' Wonderful! In the toys, games, and puzzles field, however, this definition most often fails in respect to ''both having reasonable knowledge.'' Transactions rarely are conducted on this basis. In the majority of instances the seller has far more knowledge than the buyer. If the buyer is an advanced collector, the advantage may rest with him. The knowledge scale balances less than 5 percent of the time, by my estimate.

Further, the price of any toy, game, or puzzle depends on a combination of factors, the ratio of which differs in every instance. What follows is a discussion of the factors to be considered when evaluating the price of any toy, game, or puzzle. The importance that you assign to each rests entirely with you. The rule that governs is: *there are no rules*. Mix and match to your heart's content.

Condition

Condition influences price more than anything else. Because of mass production, large numbers of each toy, game, and puzzle survive. This allows the collector to set far higher standards than when dealing with one-of-a-kind objects. Learning to adhere to high condition standards is one of the hardest tasks facing any collector. The faster you learn to do it, the faster your collection grows with premium quality items.

In the 1980s a number of leading auctioneers and writers began developing a condition grading scale for use by toy collectors. It is a major first step. Unfortunately, there is no governing body to insist on consistency. As a result, slight but very important variations exist in the condition codes. You must be alert and determine exactly which grading scale is being used. The following four grading scales, one from an auctioneer, two from mail auctioneers, and one from a writer, serve to illustrate this point.

- Hake's Americana & Collectibles

  Note: Hake does not use the "C" designation that other graders do. However, his terms and definitions correspond closely to the "C-code" systems.

  Mint: Flawless condition, like new; usually applied to items made of metal.

  Near Mint (NM): The slightest detectable wear, but appearance is still like new.

  Excellent (EXC): Only the slightest detectable wear, if any at all; usually applied to buttons, paper and other non-metallic items; also used for metallic items that just miss the near mint or mint level.

  Very Fine (VF): Bright, clean condition; an item that has seen little use and was well cared for, with only very minor wear or aging.

  Fine: An item in nice condition, with some general wear but no serious defects.

  Very Good (VG): Shows use but no serious defect, and is still nice for display; metal items may have luster or paint wear; paper items may have some small tears or creases.

  Good: May have some obvious overall wear and/or some specific defects, but still retains some collectible value.

  Fair: Obvious damage to some extent.

  Poor: Extensive damage or wear.

- New England Auction Gallery

  C10: Mint.

  C9: Near mint.

  C8: Shows light general wear.

  C7: Shows definite wear; toy may have spot(s) of corrosion; box may have tears or missing flaps.

  C6: Fine; item has some significant defect(s), but still is presentable.

  C5: Very good; item has been played with or carelessly handled.

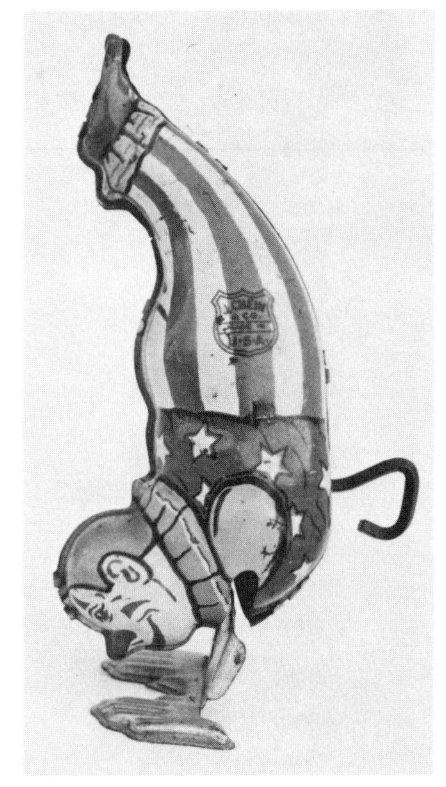

Fig. 3-1 This Chein toy shows enough signs of wear to give a maximum grade of C5.

  C4: Good; item not presentable, showing rust, stains, etc.

- Richard O'Brien, *Collecting Toys: A Collector's Identification & Value Guide, No. 5* (Note: Mint in box commands a higher price).

  C10: Mint; like new.

  C9: Near mint; no noticeable flaws, but close inspection may show minute marks.

  C8: Excellent; minor wear on edges only.

  C7: Very fine; minor wear overall; very clean.

  C6: Fine; shows some wear in spots, but taken care of.

  C5: Good; wear evident over all, showing that it has been played with.

- Lloyd Ralston Toys
    - C10: Mint in box.
    - C9: Mint.
    - C8: Near mint in box.
    - C7: Near mint.
    - C6: Excellent.
    - C5:Very fine.
    - C4: Fine.
    - C3: Very good.
    - C2: Good.
    - C1: Poor.

Check the four listings to see where they rank "fine." It is fifth from the top on Hake's list, C6 on the New England Auction Gallery list, C6 on Richard O'Brien's list, and C4 on Lloyd Ralston's list. Yet, when you compare the definitions of "fine," they are surprisingly close.

Despite the inconsistencies, several important conclusions can be drawn from these lists. First, the field makes minute but critical distinctions for examples of the best quality. Although the difference between mint and near mint may be minor, the value may double. Half of every scale is committed to grading less than 30 percent of the examples that have survived. The higher the grade, the higher the price. The temptation and pressure to overgrade is enormous.

Second, the smart collector buys nothing below fine grade. Take a hint from Richard O'Brien's book. He provides three prices for each object: C6, C8, and C10. Serious collectors avoid average examples whenever possible and shun everything below that.

Third, there are no condition grading services for toys, games, and puzzles as there are for coins and stamps. Likewise, there are no books with illustrations or charts to explain grading subtleties. (Here's an idea: a consortium of ambitious collectors could grade a toy, game, or puzzle and then seal or case so it would not be exposed to further deterioration. Would collectors or dealers support this? How about it, folks?)

How then is a condition grade assigned? It is usually assigned by the seller, hardly a disinterested individual. The only recourse you have as a collector is to develop your own standards and learn to apply them. Make them as strict as possible.

The most misused condition grading term for toys, games, and puzzles is "Mint in the Box" (MIB). It is a myth; it does not exist. MIB means that the object was never removed from the box, and neither the toy nor box was ever touched by human hands. Ideally, both should be in the exact condition that they came off the assembly line. It is all right to breathe on them, but that is all.

Let's be honest. No toy, game, or puzzle can meet this criterion. You should not expect it. Every toy, game, and puzzle is handled at some time or another. In the strictest sense, both the toy and box must be untouched to be MIB. Even if the toy were never removed from the box, exposing the box to air for a number of years alters its appearance enough to preclude the MIB designation.

A collector's search for the MIB example of his favorite toy, game, or puzzle is akin to the Knights of the Roundtable searching for the Holy Grail. They never found it; you never will, either. You can dream, but do not fail to wake up.

Cross-Market Appeal

Most toys, games, and puzzles appeal to more than one group of collectors. In this sense, the items are multifaceted. It also means that they have multiple prices. Each collector is willing to pay a different price to buy the same toy.

For example, consider a Marx B.O. Plenty lithograph tin windup toy that walks while his hat tips up and down. B.O. Plenty is a character from the Dick Tracy comic strip. B.O. has brown hair and a beard. He is dressed in a yellow shirt and hat, orange tie, blue vest, and brown pants with white strips. He holds Sparkle Plenty, his daughter, on his right arm. What collector groups have an interest in this doll? Dick Tracy collectors, B.O.

Fig. 3-2 Both the Marx collector and the Disney collector will compete for this Pinocchio toy.

Plenty collectors, Sparkle Plenty collectors, doll collectors (as a complement to Sparkle Plenty doll manufactured by Ideal), cartoon character collectors, Marx toy collectors, windup toy collectors, mechanical action toy collectors, and 1940s period collectors. There are probably others. The point is that every one of these collectors has a different value in mind in respect to the worth of the B.O. Plenty toy.

Multiplicity of value can originate outside and inside a collecting category. The doorstop collector might be able to outbid an animal collector for an animal theme doorstop. He in turn is likely to be outbid by Aunt Jemima and black memorabilia collectors, Halloween collectors, nursery rhyme theme collectors, or sports theme collectors for a doorstop crossing over into one of these categories. A child's Hopalong Cassidy cowboy hat made by Bailey of Hollywood in the early 1950s sparks competition within the western collectibles category from the general collector, Hoppy collector, TV collector, and B-movie collector. Once again, each may be willing to pay a vastly different price for the hat.

It is important to understand the multiplicity of values inherent in every toy, game, and puzzle. If you can think of only one or two potential collectors, you have not thought hard enough. Three or four is usually the minimum number. Six or more is not uncommon.

Conducting such an analysis forces you to recognize your competition and reach firm conclusions on how much the toy is worth to you. Since there are so many factors influencing price, the only price that you should care about is the one that you are willing to pay. If something is priced higher than that, do not pay it no matter how much you may want the toy. Easy to say, very hard to do!

Completeness and Playability

Defining an "original" toy, game, or puzzle should be simple: it is exactly as it came from the assembly line. But an assembly line implies interchangeability. If a toy that is missing a part is repaired with an original part from an identical toy, is it any less original? For example, it is occasionally possible to switch pieces between die-cut cardboard puzzles to make one complete puzzle out of two incomplete ones. "Original," then, must be defined loosely. As long as all the parts constituting the object are from the initial period of its production, it can be considered original.

Similarly, it is possible for a toy or game to consist of original parts, but not be complete. When an original part is missing from a puzzle, it is rather evident. Completeness is critical; a toy, game, or puzzle that is not complete has a lower value.

Determining the completeness of toys and

games is not as easy as it sounds. You have the best chance with games, since most instruction sheets provide exact piece counts. Game collectors discipline themselves to check, which is why you see them carefully counting pieces at flea markets, malls, shops, and shows. Do not be deceived by ease of substitution. Replacing the proper dice for a track board game with an incorrect pair can lower value 5 to 10 percent.

The problem with toys is that they are rarely documented. Early catalogs contained hand-drawn line illustrations. When photographs finally replaced these, most catalogs showed only one side of a toy or toys in groups. Manufacturers rarely took production photographs. How then do you know if a toy is complete? The answer is by examining as many surviving examples as possible. Look for subtle differences. Make notes—memory is a tricky commodity.

Once you have determined that a toy, game, or puzzle is original and complete, the final step is to make certain that you can play with it. If a toy or game relies on mechanical action, it has to work. If it does not work, value decreases by up to 50 percent.

Restoration: When and How Much?

The toy, game, and puzzle field is fraught with ambiguous terms. While "repaired," "rebuilt," "restored," and "conserved" technically have specific meanings, they are used interchangeably by collectors and dealers alike. After reading this section, you should be less confused than most.

View these terms as "warning triggers." When you hear them, go on the alert and carefully examine the toy, game, or puzzle that you are considering buying. Each term conveys one simple fact: some portion of the object is no longer original. In no instance, no matter how much the surviving piece looks like the original, should you pay the price of an original. A commonly used cliche is "better than new." Do not believe it; it is another myth.

"Repaired" means an object has been made presentable, i.e., restored to good condition. In many cases, little effort is made to make the repair conform to the original in respect to either shape or color. While a repair may not be readily apparent from a distance, it usually is from arm's length. Although repairs may enhance the appearance of a toy, game, or puzzle somewhat, they raise the value only slightly—10 to 15 percent—from that of an unrepaired toy. Never pay a premium for something crudely done.

"Rebuilt" means reconstructed. The key is whether the toy is reconstructed from original or new parts. The distinction is important, even though there are some excellent new replacement parts on the market. The piece rebuilt with original parts is worth more than the piece rebuilt with modern replacement parts.

Collectors and dealers will acquire toys, games, and puzzles in extremely bad condition if some portions of the object can be used for spare parts. Unlike the automobile industry, few toy, game, or puzzle manufacturers have a spare parts distribution system. The only source for spares are examples too far gone to be repaired. One major problem with the condition grading scales discussed previously is that none of them includes a grade for a "parts" toy, game, or puzzle. One generally expects to pay about 5 percent of book value for a parts toy if 10 to 25 percent of the toy can be salvaged. If the salvage percentage is higher, so is the price. In no case should the price exceed 10 percent of book value.

Whenever possible, seek examples rebuilt with original parts. Since the finished product is identical to the original, such rebuilding is often not mentioned by the seller. Ethically, it should be. Alas, the same situation often holds true when newly made parts are used to rebuild the toy. Some of the replacement parts presently available are almost impossible to tell from their original counterparts.

Fig. 3-3 The wheels on this Hubley toy appear to have been rebuilt. This lowers its value by more than 50 percent.

In order not to be deceived, you must set up two lines of defense. First, you should maintain a file of all catalogs listing replacement parts. Supplement this information by visits to toy shows where the parts can be inspected and handled. Whenever you see a toy that has a part corresponding to one of the replacement parts, alarm bells should ring. Second, you must be aggressive in asking a seller if any rebuilding work was done on the item you are considering purchasing. Learn to do it in every instance, no matter what you have concluded after inspecting the object.

"Restored" refers to an example that has been repaired, rebuilt, or altered so that it resembles the original as closely as possible. The work is skillfully done, usually by someone who specializes in repairing and rebuilding toys, games, or puzzles. It is not uncommon for a restorer to actually make missing parts from scratch. The work is done so that the repair or rebuilding is noticeable only upon very close inspection. Some individuals find it challenging to do restoration that is not noticeable at all. These should frighten you.

"Conserved" represents the highest standards of restoration. There are two key differences that separate the conservation process from the restoration process. First, conservation work is done by trained professionals. Such training includes undergraduate and graduate college or university degrees, plus serving an apprenticeship for a minimum of two years. Conservators generally are used only on museum-quality pieces because their hourly rates are similar to those charged by attorneys and accountants. Second, conservators are extremely cautious about what they do. Everything is carefully documented. Nothing is done that cannot be undone at a later date. Many refuse to hide repairs so that they cannot be seen. You may not see them at arm's length, but you will at close inspection.

A major problem involving repairers and restorers is that there is no training or licensing system. As a collector, one of the most important things you must do is identify individuals you consider talented enough to work on objects in your collection. Closely study examples of their work. Check references carefully. Poor quality work is one thing; damage to a piece that cannot be restored is another. Both happen.

For these reasons, most collectors prefer buying toys, games, and puzzles "as-is." They recognize that it is better to have their own sources do the repairing, rebuilding, or restoring. This presents a dilemma for the seller. If a toy, game, or puzzle needing work is sold "as-is," the price is lower. With a little effort, the value can be raised considerably. In many cases, the seller proceeds full-steam ahead, the collector's wishes be damned.

Every seller is ethically bound to reveal to the buyer any repair, rebuilding, restoration, or conservation work. The burden is then placed on the buyer to decide how to interpret it. If the work is unsatisfactory, the buyer must calculate the cost of redoing it. This cost should be figured in to the asking price of the toy, game, or puzzle to arrive at its actual cost. In many cases, the cost of redoing a poor job may exceed the asking price.

The status of any toy, game, or puzzle should be spelled out specifically on the sales receipt. If an object has been repaired, rebuilt, or restored and that information is not revealed to the buyer and specified on the sales receipt, a strong case can be made that the object was misrepresented, which should never be tolerated.

Toy, game, and puzzle collectors place tremendous emphasis on originality. However, a dangerous shift in attitude is occurring in some parts of the market, most noticeably among wheeled vehicle collectors. These collectors are accepting "restored to original condition" as equal to or better than original.

The concept originated with collectors of antique, classic, and vintage cars. Total wrecks are rebuilt from the frame up. Great liberties are taken as many missing parts are newly manufactured and old paint and other finishes copied. Although they may look original, some of the cars that win gold medals at car shows are less than 50 percent original. These standards may satisfy the car collector, but they should never satisfy the toy, game, or puzzle collector.

You cannot restore anything to original condition. At best, you can restore it to look like the original. In your mind, there should be a big difference between "restored to original" and "original". Anything that blurs this distinction is a direct threat to the order that currently governs practices in the toys, games, and puzzles area. Repairing, rebuilding, restoring, or conserving should never restore full value to anything. The highest price must be reserved for objects in their original, unaltered state.

Collectors become known by the quality of the toys they buy. It is important that from the beginning you establish a reputation of being a discriminating buyer by insisting that the objects you buy are of the highest quality and integrity. If you become known as someone who will accept second-rate material, this is all that you will be offered. Let someone else be duped; you know better.

Original Paint

Toy, game, and puzzle collectors are obsessed with finding ways to rank the top pieces in each specific collecting category. Collectors are fiercely competitive. They are driven by the desire to own the "best example known." Dealers play along because of the tremendously high prices involved. When you understand this, you can better put it into perspective.

While the serious collector may recognize the phenomenon, the media and the general public do not. The media loves reporting upbeat, record price stories. The more spectacular the price realized, the more widely disseminated the story. The general public reads these stories and gets the mistaken impression that every toy, game, or puzzle has high potential value. Every collector and dealer spends a great deal of time telling would-be sellers from the general public that their objects are only worth a fraction of what they think.

A great deal of responsibility for this problem rests with the "original paint fanatics" in the mechanical bank, cast iron, and tin toy area. Collectors and dealers alike devote endless hours to calculating the percentage of original paint left on a toy. They have accepted without question the premise that the higher the percentage of original paint, the higher the value.

How can you determine the percentage of original paint with any degree of accuracy? The surface area of most toys is irregular, so any figure is nothing more than an educated guess. Further, percentage of original paint is hardly good enough. Paint changes over time due to oxidation, patination, chemical shifts, and a host of other causes. If value is going to be based on the percentage of paint, shouldn't equal weight be given to the per-

Fig. 3-4 If this Tootsietoy were repainted, over two-thirds of its value would be gone.

centage by which the color remains true to the original? How absurd do we want to become?

Prices begin to escalate rapidly in the original paint school when percentage calculations reach 90 percent and beyond. A piece with 90 percent original paint will sell for two to four times book value for a C8 (excellent) piece. Prices double or triple again between 90 and 95 percent. Value beyond the average collectors' wildest belief comes into play when original paint reaches the 98 percent and higher mark. A mechanical bank that sells at fine condition for $750 has the potential to realize $50,000 or more at 98 percent original paint.

The amount of money involved removes most collectors from playing the "original paint" game. It is at best a risky business. Opinions change. If a toy is downgraded even a few percentage points, the drop in value involves thousands of dollars. The easiest way to avoid this is not to support the "original paint fanatics." Given the amount of money involved, it should not be difficult.

Original Box

What did you do with the boxes that your toys came in? Threw them out, right? So did virtually everyone else. That is why, in many cases, boxes can be worth as much or more than the toy.

Stop and think for a moment. How many Mickey Mouse watches have you seen for sale? Now, how many Mickey Mouse watch boxes have you seen? For an example of how value is affected, let's consult Howard S. Brenner's *Collecting Comic Character Clocks and Watches: Identification And Value Guide* (Books Americana, 1987). A 1950 Ingersoll (U.S. Time) Mickey Mouse wrist watch books for $50 mint and $200 MIB. A 1950 U.S. Time Hopalong Cassidy wrist watch, leather band, is valued at $50 mint and $150 if accompanied by its original "saddle stand" box. The average increase in value of clocks and watches listed in Brenner's book is 50 to 100 percent between a mint watch and a mint watch with its box. Does it pay to save the box? You bet it does.

"Box" is used in a very broad context. Packaging is the correct term. Many toys, games, and puzzles were not merchandised in boxes. Cellophane wrap, blister packs, and plastic bags are just a few of the other techniques. The original cellophane wrap on the first GI Joe doll adds $1,000 to its value.

The box is an integral part of the presentation of every toy, game, and puzzle. Even if the box only contains the name of the toy and its manufacturer, it has value. Many boxes picture the object, often in an idyllic setting. Other information may include name and address of manufacturer, copyright and licensing data, premium offers, and instructions for use. If the box contains any of this information, a toy, game, or puzzle is incomplete without it.

In the case of early games and, to some extent, puzzles, the box may be the most critical element. Game and puzzle boxes of the late 19th and early 20th century featured some of the finest lithography done in America. Collectors view the boxes as works of art. Collectors will accept loss of game parts and puzzle pieces much more easily than they will accept damage to the box. Even collectors of post-World War II games and puzzles recognize the importance of the box and insist not only that it be present, but in very good or better condition.

How much does the original box add to the value? Here are a few general rules for determining value of an original box for toys, games, and puzzles: a 100 percent increase for toys, games, and puzzles from 1850 to 1915, 50 to 60 percent for examples from 1916 to 1940, and 30 to 40 percent for examples since 1940. Use only one-quarter of these percentages if the box is plain; use one-half of these percentages if the picture on the box is not an exact duplicate of either the toy or the person or thing the toy is meant to represent. Rules, however, are meant to be broken. These percentages are only guides. What is the box worth? We have already discussed the definition of value.

The importance of the original box has been recognized for the past decade. Collectors now accept the concept without question. The potential value of original internal packaging is another matter. There is no consensus of opinion about this. There is a growing recognition that when it is present, it should increase value, but no one is exactly certain by how much. Current guesses range from a few percentage points to as much as 10 to 15 percent.

The box is becoming a collectible in its own right. Many boxes are extremely decorative. A major market development of the 1980s was the recognition that many toys, games, and puzzles had a "decorator value" vastly different from their worth in the established marketplace. The concept is known as the "PS Quotient." I explain it in detail in my *How to Make the Most of Your Investments in Antiques and Collectibles* (Arbor House, 1988). "P" stands for pizzazz value; "S" indicates snob appeal.

Another force that creates independent value for the box is its portrayal of a famous cartoon, movie, radio, or television personality. I make this point reluctantly, because when value of this nature is created, there is a strong tendency among dealers to separate the box from the toy, game, or puzzle that it housed to sell it independently. Collectors resent the time and money they must spend to put back together things that started out life as a single unit.

Since the original box plays such an important role in assessing the completeness of toys, games, and puzzles, it is extremely important to know its condition when making a purchase. The condition of a box may differ greatly from the toy housed in it. Because grading box condition is in its infancy, assigned grades, whether by collector or dealer, tend to be very generous. Tougher standards are needed. Several auctioneers and dealers have recently begun dual condition grading. Their efforts are applauded; it is a major step in the right direction.

In addition to the box and packaging, be alert for any inserts, such as instruction sheets, mini-

Fig. 3-5 The graphics on the box for this Charlie McCarthy and Mortimer Snerd Coupe are superb. The toy is simply not complete unless it is present.

catalogs, and premium offers. Cocomalt's 1932 "Flying Family" advertising jigsaw puzzles originally contained a four-page brochure on how to become a flight commander. If it is missing, the value of the puzzle is decreased by 25 percent. Because of poor records, it is difficult to know what, if any, inserts were part of the original packaging. This is one area where shared knowledge among collectors is essential.

The Sum of the Parts

An increasingly common practice in the collectibles field is the separation of units into their component parts for resale. In the 1980s Scott Bruce demonstrated that you could increase the value of a lunch kit by 50 percent or more simply by separating the box from the thermos and selling them separately. Bruce did not originate the practice; it had been going on quietly for decades.

I'm not naive. No collector expects to find every toy, game, and puzzle intact. As individuals played with them, parts and pieces were lost or broken. Remaining parts have value, especially when they can be used to recreate a complete unit. But the key question is, should their value be greater than the complete unit?

The practice of breaking up toys, games, and puzzles has many roots. The foremost is greed, the desire to milk the last ounce of value out of every object. No one objects to an honest profit, but a greedy profit is something else entirely.

Yet specialized collectors often become frustrated with complete sets when only one item in the set holds any interest for them. For example, the Auburn Rubber Roy Rogers Ranger Set contained a rubber pocket knife, hunting knife, pistol, and tomahawk. The collector of children's pistols is interested only in the pistol, not the rest. He may be willing to pay one-third to one-half the value of the set to get the pistol. He saves money, and the set is broken up.

There are plenty of examples in the games and puzzles category. A number of articles have been written recently about collecting game playing boards. They look great hanging on the wall. Collectors have been known to buy a game intact, keep the board, and throw the rest in the trash. Puzzle sets are broken up when the puzzles picture an animal, cartoon character, or personality. If you

Fig. 3-6 The Today Show game features playing pieces in the shape of miniature TV cameras. They often show up at flea markets for sale independent of the board game.

sell the four Popeye puzzles from the 1932 Saalfield set independently, you double the value. Add another $30 to $50 for the box.

Disassembling a toy, game, or puzzle and selling its component parts is deplorable. Individuals who do this deserve our strongest condemnation and contempt. They should be shunned; the darkest place in hell should be reserved as their resting place. Now, if there were only a worldly penalty!

The blame does not rest solely on dealers—collectors have to share it. Dealers would stop the practice if collectors would refuse to buy toys, games, and puzzles that are not complete, or refuse to pay premium prices for parts. But collectors themselves are out of control. Their desire to own frequently overwhelms their common sense.

This problem wreaks havoc when trying to determine the value of a collection. Collectors demand a premium. They add up the value of each unit and then increase this figure by a percentage, usually 50 percent or more, to come up with a value for the collection as a whole. This is the reason many collections are broken up and sold at auction. After repeated failure to negotiate a selling price, collectors wake up to the reality that the maximum return is achieved only when the parts are sold individually.

Fig. 3-7 Boy Scout collectibles avoid crazes because the market is narrowly controlled by a specialized group of collectors and dealers.

Crazes and Fads

The value of toys, games, and puzzles is very much influenced by crazes that can take place within a specific category, the antiques and collectibles market as a whole, and areas outside the market. This is why so much talk among collectors and dealers concerns what is hot and what is not. The fact that values can change dramatically, sometimes overnight, requires a great deal of flexibility.

The wise collector must understand the *hows* and *whys* that drive the market. Crazes and trends can be predicted. Recognizing where the market is at any given moment leads to responsible and prudent action. You will find the first eight chapters of my book, *How to Make the Most of Your Investments in Antiques and Collectibles* (New York: Arbor House, 1988), especially helpful in this regard.

No category of antiques and collectibles enjoys a steady increase in prices. Rather, price increases occur cataclysmically. When an item gets hot, prices tend to double, triple, and even quadruple in a very short period. It is a wild time. Many collectors are turned off and drop out. The smart collector learns how to ride out the storm.

The key is learning to adjust one's thinking. All too often collectors remember what they paid for something five or 10 years ago. That price may have absolutely no validity in today's market. This is not to argue for blind acceptance of price increases—things can become overpriced. There is

Fig. 3-8 In the mid-1970s Disneyana went crazy. Now the market has become so sophisticated that crazes within the Disney market occur by individual character.

a fine line between a high price and a ridiculous price.

As individual collecting categories become more sophisticated, the crazes that occur become narrower. The toy, game, and puzzle markets are excellent examples. It is impossible to talk about a single toy, game, or puzzle market. The toy market has more than 10 major subdivisions (e.g., tin, lithographed tin, cast iron, windup, battery-operated, character, etc.). Some toys fit in more than one subdivision: a lithographed tin, battery-operated toy is one example.

There are a number of events inside and outside the market that can trigger a craze. Inside triggers include advice from experts, books, magazine and newspaper articles, museum exhibits, single-owner auction sales, and the field itself. Decorator and fashion trends, investor publications, television, and calendar and political events constitute outside triggers. Not everything works as a trigger. By being alert to the potential, you are prepared for action.

Market Manipulation

Market manipulation in the toys, games, and puzzles sector is not new. It simply became more open in the 1980s. Before 1980 the most common method of manipulating the market was to write a price guide about the toys one had collected, publish it, and sell the collection within a year or two after publication. The author usually had devoted a decade or more to assemblying his or her collection. Prices in the book in no way reflected what the author paid; they represented what the author thought each toy should be worth. Rarely were these prices questioned. In many cases, the book stimulated interest in the category, forcing prices even higher. The increase was supported by dealers, who took pleasure in challenging price guide prices.

In the 1980s market manipulators added speed and breadth to the process. Collections were built in months or a few years through aggressive buying and advertising. The media, museums, and collectors—especially collectors' newsletters and clubs—were used to fan the flames. Prices in a number of categories, such as McLoughlin board games, monster theme toys, friction toys, and pedal cars, went crazy.

What upset many collectors and dealers was the brazenness of the manipulators. They made no secret of what they were doing. In fact, they flaunted it. As long as money flowed freely and everyone got rich, no one seemed to care. In 1990 the tide began to turn. Collectors and dealers began to express resentment toward market manipulators. Individuals now working on a second or third manipulation within 10 years are finding tough sledding.

Market manipulation benefits no one except the manipulator and the first individuals to sell their collections during the price run. High prices caused by manipulation effectively shut off a category to new collectors. When prices do collapse—and they do—a bitter taste is left. Collectors who joined the craze for the short run find they are in for the long term.

Market manipulation is not done just by individuals. A consortium of dealers can achieve the same end by fixing prices and working a number of well-heeled collectors. While it would be virtually impossible to prove that a conspiracy to fix prices exists in the toy, game, and puzzle field, one cannot help but notice how often the same toy, game, or puzzle is identically priced in the booths of established dealers in the trade. This is why smart collectors shop the common material. Eventually, they find someone who is not tuned into the game.

Be extremely suspicious if a dealer who is supplying you with material is slowly increasing the price on each piece being offered. You are being worked. Sometimes manipulation focuses on one individual. In my first year of puzzle collecting, I met a dealer who had a number of outstanding advertising puzzles at top market value. I bought them. Soon, other quality puzzles were offered to me over the telephone. I bought them, too. Finally, the dealer called with a rather common advertising puzzle at a rather uncommon price. I turned it down. A week later another common puzzle was offered for $125. Its market value was in the $25 to $40 range. I again turned it down. One of my pickers visited this dealer's booth at an antiques show and was offered the same puzzle quoted to me at $125 for $35. I found out about it, and the dealer lost a valuable customer. I will never do business with her again.

The adverse reaction to market manipulators of all types is most welcome. The one disadvantage is that the manipulators are being driven underground. To survive, manipulators will find new methods to disguise their techniques, so you must remain vigilant.

Affordability

Is it possible to price something out of the market? Theoretically, the answer is "no." The toy, game, and puzzle field is blessed with a number of very rich collectors. In reality, however, the answer is "yes." When the common toys, games, and puzzles in any subcategory begin selling in the $100-plus range, the average collector is left out.

Toys, games, and puzzles have always been one of the chief avenues for attracting new collectors to the antiques and collectibles field. There are plenty of opportunities to purchase great material for a few cents to a few dollars. Until the 1980s the inexpensive portion of the toys, games, and puzzles field covered material manufactured over the past 40 years. The toys, games, and puzzles of one's youth were both plentiful and affordable. "Serious" collectors focused on earlier material, but even there prices in the hundreds, not thousands, were common.

The greed of the 1980s affected collector and dealer alike. The price difference between the top pieces and the bottom pieces kept getting wider and wider. Common pieces were pulled up in price by ever-increasing prices at the top. Suddenly, the top end of the toy market jumped to tens and even hundreds of thousands of dollars, the top end of the game market to tens of thousands, and the top end of the puzzle market to the high hundreds and low thousands.

The search for affordable material led collectors to focus on the toys, games, and puzzles of the 1940 to 1970 period. Before one could say "shazam" prices were in the high tens and hundreds of dollars for this material. The toy, game, and puzzle market went on a roll, which continues to some extent even as this book is being written.

Fig. 3-9 Advertising jigsaw puzzles are still affordable. But will they be in 10 years?

However, the potential repercussions are frightening. The entry level collector is now buying toys, games, and puzzles from the 1970s and 1980s. Under Rinker's Thirty-Year Rule, all the values related to this material are speculative. Rumors of hard times ahead are rampant in the field. If they are true, the common, above average, and hard-to-find-but-available toys, games, and puzzles from 1920 to 1970 are going to be very hard hit. Any toy, game, or puzzle subgroup that experienced a major price jump in the 1980s is vulnerable.

No book has been written devoted exclusively to discussing the factors that influence value among antiques and collectibles, although there is reason enough for doing so. You are probably thinking: "I'll never be able to sort this out. Why bother to collect toys, games, or puzzles at all? I'll choose a less complicated antiques or collectibles category."

The answer is twofold. First, no matter what category of antiques and collectibles you choose, the above factors apply. In fact, there may be even more. Second, FUN, FUN, FUN! The joy of collecting is the joy of collecting. Go at it with that purpose alone, and you will never regret it.

Back to business.

Other Factors

Research

The more you know about a toy, game, or puzzle, the higher its value. Research adds value. The six key questions that every collector wants to know about a toy, game, or puzzle are:

1. Who designed it?
2. Who made it?
3. When was it made?
4. In what variations was it made?
5. How many were made?
6. How long was it made?

For most toys, games, and puzzles, the only questions for which specific answers are generally known are 2 and 3. The identity of the designer is one of the hardest pieces of information to obtain. The question of variation is important because it relates to scarcity. Hard-to-find variations usually command higher prices. If the truth were known about quantity of production, value concepts for toys, games, and puzzles would change dramatically. Perhaps this question is best left unanswered. Finally, one must be careful to distinguish the final date of production from the final date of distribution. Many toys, games, and puzzles were distributed for years after production ceased.

One area where collectors make a major contribution to the toys, games, and puzzles field is through the preparation of checklists. The lists may focus on a company's products (Fisher-Price or Marx), or theme (Hopalong Cassidy collectibles or Depression-era puzzles), or type (bobbin' head dolls). Many of these checklists become books. However, the vast majority are circulated privately among collectors.

Why are checklists so important? Collectors are timid. They like to collect what they know. Checklists make them comfortable; they tell them exactly what to seek. Do not rely too heavily on checklists. Assume no checklist is complete. Likewise, do not fall prey to the oft-touted concept that since a toy, game, or puzzle is not illustrated in a book or on a checklist, it is rare and, therefore, should command a high price. The person preparing the list may have inadvertently left it off, or simply missed it altogether.

Dare to lead. If you find a toy, game, or puzzle subcategory that you love and no one else is collecting it, collect it. Be a pioneer. The only person you need to justify your collecting to is yourself.

Although the toy, game, and puzzle market appears to be endless, it subdivides into hundreds of specialized interests. The Man from U.N.C.L.E. collector has virtually no interest in Gunsmoke collectibles. Within each specialized collecting group, the number of serious players is relatively small. Rarely does that number exceed one hundred. The number of top players—those who pay top dollar for the top items—usually can be counted on one hand.

The Hoard

Every dealer and collector lives in fear that somewhere is a warehouse filled with hundreds of examples of the lead toy, game, or puzzle in his collection. The fear is real because warehouse finds happen. If the find is small, little or no effect is felt in the marketplace. If the hoard is large, as it often is, the market is affected adversely.

Hoards are discovered all the time. Collectors and dealers flock to sales of old grocery and country stores, pharmacies, and warehouses. They write manufacturers asking to buy discontinued merchandise and advertising material. When one company acquires another, the acquired company's product and advertising archives are often discarded. Collectors and dealers line up by the trash bin. Finally, some farsighted collectors buy a quantity of material when it is first produced, store it for 10 to 30 years, and finally release it into the market. Every year in November I spend $200 on toys, games, and puzzles that I put into storage. In 30 years, I will turn them over to my children to sell. If I selected well, the return will far exceed the amount I would have received had I put the money into a savings institution.

Fig. 3-10 One of 10 copies of the same jigsaw puzzle seen at a dealer's booth.

Market value is threatened by any hoard greater than 40 pieces. Given that most hoards are warehouse finds, the objects tend to be in excellent or better condition. The seller of the hoard expects top dollar. This does not deter collectors who already own an example. They welcome the opportunity to upgrade. If someone finds a hoard consisting of hundreds or thousands of objects, they are well advised to destroy most of them. It might be sacrilegious, but it is good business sense.

How do you spot a hoard? There are three clues: sudden appearance of merchandise in quantity, its condition, and its price. After you have been collecting for several years, you develop a good comprehension of the range of toys, games, and puzzles in your specialized collecting field. Seeing a unknown example at a flea market, mall, shop, or show for the first time causes the adrenalin to flow. Be careful. Put a hold on it and make a sweep of the area. If the object is part of a hoard, chances are great that you will see another.

Children played with their toys, games, and puzzles. Collectors are used to finding signs of use. When an example is seen in unused condition, do not think "act of God," think "hoard." Do not be deceived by water-stained or mildewed packaging. This is storage damage, not use damage, and is often a sign of a warehouse hoard.

Price is the hardest way to spot a hoard. The individual who controls the hoard may selectively test the market by selling a few high priced examples to recoup his initial investment and make a fair profit. Once satisfied that he has milked the market, he will dump the rest. Two results are possible: market prices become depressed, or prices stabilize at a value of little or no appeal to the collector. A hoard of Nabisco Straight Arrow puzzles entered the market in mid-1989. Initial pricing was in the $10 to $15 range. With sales brisk, the balance of the hoard was put on the market. Dealers gobbled them up. They are now priced in the $30.00 to $45.00 range, and no one is buying them.

Sometimes a single collection can constitute a hoard. It took Noel Barrett Antiques & Auctions Ltd. three major catalog sales to disperse the Gottschalk toy collection. Toys in the third sale did not perform as well as identical toys in the first two sales. The collection created temporary market flooding in some categories. Record prices paid at the first two sales depleted the spending power of some key collectors. Identify collectors with extremely large collections as quickly as possible after you start collecting in a specialized area. Become friends with the owner and keep on top of his long-term plans for the material.

Finally, a number of unscrupulous dealers are disguising reproductions, copycat, and fantasy items as "warehouse finds." Since licensing information is not known, many collectors and dealers are being suckered by these shysters. Beware of anyone offering to sell pre-1960s material in quantities of 10 or more.

The Oldest

American collectors place great value on owning the oldest or first model of any toy, game, or puzzle. Because of the lack of records, these claims are frequently open to question. The earliest known example or the first model of any toy, game, or puzzle does deserve an honored place. Does it also deserve an honored price? If possible, divorce yourself from the aura and examine the toy, game, or puzzle objectively. Is it the best-made example? Does it have pizzazz? Is it a highly collectible theme? In almost every instance, the answer to these questions is "no." Enough said.

Collectors must also resist the temptation to value something simply because it is old. Remember, *a 100-year-old piece of manure is not an antique, it is a 100-year-old piece of horse—*. If the piece cannot stand on its own merit, excluding the age consideration, it does not deserve an honored place or an honored price.

This view defies the traditional logic of the toy, game, and puzzle market. Assigning the highest value to the oldest and first is one of the field's most sacred cows. You choose whether or not you wish to accept it.

Regional Value

A standard rule in the antiques and collectibles trade is: "Take a product back to its place of origin and double its value." Collectors in the toy, game, and puzzle market who focus only on the toys, games, and puzzles produced in their locality must face the truth: The rule does not apply to them.

The toy, game, and puzzle market is national, if not international. Regional collectors face enormous competition for the toys from their region from collectors outside their region. The regional collector who pays top dollar for a toy only because it was manufactured locally should ask himself how familiar the seller is with his collecting interest. Is he being exploited?

Prominent Ownership

Does a toy, game, or puzzle gain additional value because it was owned by a famous personality or was part of a leading collection? The answer, which should be "no," is "yes." It is common practice to assign a 10 to 25 percent value increase to a toy, game, or puzzle that meets these criteria. Every collector should be concerned with the temporal nature of these values.

You must question everything. No, it does not turn you into the world's biggest skeptic. It turns you into the world's shrewdest collector. Two

Fig. 3-11 Suprisingly enough, this SOHIO advertising jigsaw puzzle has less value in Ohio, where the puzzle is plentiful, than in the rest of the country, where it is not.

questions should be asked here: (1) What makes the person famous, and in 20 years will anyone care? (2) What proof do you have to offer that this is the actual piece from the collection?

How do you determine if someone is famous? Ask 50 people if they can identify the person. Want to have some fun? Try Ed Wynn and Hopalong Cassidy. You will be surprised at the results. The old adage states, "Fame is fleeting." It is correct. In the long run, everyone is forgotten. Why pay a premium for a name?

In the field of toys, games, and puzzles, claims that "it came from the Perelman Museum," "it came from the Dennis collection," and "it belonged to Gottschalk" will be bantered about as evidence that the item has special value. The key is proof. Do not trust the word of the seller. Do not trust the fact that it is pictured in the sale catalog. Do not even trust the fact it may have a label on it saying it was part of the collection.

Toys, games, and puzzles were mass produced. It is easy to substitute one example for another. What should you trust? Trust the original bill of sale if it accompanies the piece. Better yet, do not place any premium on the piece because of this type of provenance.

What is the greatest factor that influences value? The answer is "you." Never forget it.

CHAPTER 4

Buying, Trading, and Selling

For most collectors, the joy is in the collecting, not the selling. Selling material from their collections is tantamount to selling their children—unthinkable.

Yet, inevitably, most collectors join the ranks of the sellers, often becoming part-time dealers. They sell to upgrade, to rid themselves of duplicates, or simply to get the money they need to afford an example that they value more highly than one in their collection. Very few collectors remain purists who never sell and rarely trade.

One of the major developments in the toys, games, and puzzles sector in the 1980s was a surge in the number of individuals who combined collecting and dealing. One astute member of the trade observed: "Everyone is a dealer. There are no collectors left." This does not bode well. In a healthy market, collectors should outnumber dealers by 10 to 1 or more. As the 1990s begin, there are signs that a market correction is taking place.

Buying Toys, Games, and Puzzles

Toys, games, and puzzles are found at auctions, flea markets, garage sales, malls, shops, shows, and in trade newspaper advertisements. An assumption is made that you are already familiar with these sources to some extent. This section begins by focusing on auctions and shows devoted exclusively to toys, games, and puzzles. It ends with a series of hints on how to buy through the trade papers and from specialized dealers.

Auctions

In the 1980s three important auction developments occurred that affected the toy market. First, a number of local and regional auctioneers realized the potential of specialized toy auctions. They now represent formidable competition for Lloyd Ralston, the auctioneer who pioneered the specialized toy auction and enjoys a well-deserved national reputation. Second, the major New York auction houses entered the upscale side of the market. Third, a number of dealers linked up with auctioneers to conduct the sale of key private collections.

- Lloyd Ralston Toys, 447 Stratfield Rd., Fairfield, CT 06432.

Lloyd Ralston Toys is the leading auction house for toys, games, and puzzles in the United States. In the mid-1970s Ralston purchased a toy collection. Analyzing the profit he might receive from taking it to a number of toy shows, he decided to

Fig. 4-1 Before buying anything at auction, it pays to preview the material.

hold an auction. The results far exceeded his expectations, and began his auction career.

Ralston holds four to five catalog auctions each year. Every item is illustrated, condition grades are provided, and prices realized are published. Because of Ralston's excellent reputation, you can bid with confidence by mail or phone. However, you should telephone in advance and discuss the toys in which you have an interest with a number of the staff.

Lloyd Ralston Toys also sells privately through its gallery in Fairfield, Connecticut. Ralston and members of his family are frequent exhibitors at toy shows in the eastern half of the United States. Getting to know their merchandise and staff makes great sense.

- Richard Opfer Auctioneering, Inc., 1919 Green Spring Dr., Timonium, MD 21093.

Richard Opfer is known throughout the trade for his specialized auctions, ranging from advertising to black memorabilia to pharmaceutical items to toys. Not every sale has a published catalog; sometimes only a simple sale list is employed. Photographs may be used, but not every lot is pictured and descriptions vary. It pays to preview all material before bidding.

- Noel Barrett Auctions and Appraisals, P.O. Box 1001, Carversville, PA 18913.

Noel Barrett and Bill Bertoia teamed up to sell the collection of the Atlanta Toy Museum through a series of auctions in 1987 and 1988. Barrett further enhanced his auction reputation with the three cataloged auctions required to sell the Bill Gottschalk toy collection in 1990. Barrett has made his mark in the single-owner sale. To be a dominant force in the trade he will have to conduct assembled sales with equally impressive results.

- Ted Maurer, 1003 Brookwood Dr., Pottstown, PA 19464.

Ted Maurer is typical of the local auctioneer who is carving a niche in the specialized toy auction field. He runs two to three specialized toy and/or train auctions each year. His auction room is a local firehall or church. Recently, he began scheduling his sales one or two days before a major toy show in his area. The majority of the bidders are dealers, partly because much of the material is sold in lots.

- Sotheby's, 1334 York Ave., New York, NY 10021.

Twice a year, Sotheby's conducts a Carousel auction focusing on animation art, dolls, music boxes, rock and roll and movie memorabilia, and toys. Items offered are upscale: they are expected to sell in the $1000-plus range. Many meet these expectations.

- Christie's East, 219 East 67th St., New York, NY 10022.

Until 1990, Christie's East annually held one or two specialized auctions focusing on sport collectibles, movie memorabilia, and toys. Items sold from a few hundred to several thousand dollars. Christie's East was an excellent source for high quality material from the middle sector of the market. All the sales were "assembled," meaning they were not the collections of one seller. Unfortunately, increasing overhead, a problem facing all New York auction houses, has made selling items

Fig. 4-2 Toy, game, and puzzle auctions are generally well attended.

valued in the low hundreds no longer feasible. The return simply does not warrant the time involved in cataloging and selling. Christie's East will continue to hold single-owner auctions in the toy area, but no longer plans assembled toy auctions.

- Phillips New York, 406 East 79th Street, New York, NY 10021.

The decline of the house of Phillips in New York was one of the tragedies of the 1980s. It offered an important alternative to Sotheby's and Christie's, especially in the area of toys. One of its great strengths was its lead soldier sales, assembled by Henry I. Kurtz. Phillips plans to maintain its United States presence by conducting several toy soldier sales each year. They often contain other toys as well. Keep an eye open for the dates.

In regard to auction houses, American collectors often look only at American firms. This is a major mistake. Serious collectors also acquire the sale catalogs from Christie's, Phillips, and Sotheby's English and continental European houses. Many conduct one or more specialized toy auctions each year.

More and more toys, games, and puzzles are being sold through mail auctions. They differ from auctions held by auction houses in that the primary bidders are private collectors, not dealers. This means that items sell at market value and higher. They work because of the integrity of the mail auctioneers, who guarantee the return of any unsatisfactory lot, no questions asked.

The mail auctions listed below issue a catalog that pictures every lot and provides a detailed description and condition report for each lot. Catalogs are received by paying an annual fee. The key to participating in a mail auction is to understand its rules. Read the rules carefully before you preview the rest of the catalog. Follow this practice each time a mail auction catalog arrives. Rules can change from auction to auction; you must be prepared.

Bidding is done by mail and over the telephone. Telephone bidding usually takes place on the last two days of the sale. Participants call to check on their bids and raise them if they wish. Most auctions end "when 10 minutes pass without a phone call after 11PM EST" on the last day of the auction. It is not uncommon for auctions to last into the following morning.

- Hake's Americana & Collectibles, P.O. Box 1444, York, PA 17405.

Hake's Americana & Collectibles is the mail auction by which all others are judged. Hake's descriptions and condition reports are the finest in the business, outshining even the New York houses. His mailing list consists of the top collectors in the United States and abroad.

Hake conducts five to six mail auctions each year, with each auction containing about 3,000 lots. Auction results are not published, although bidders can write or call for information about the lots on which they bid. In addition, Hake issues a number of specialized immediate sale lists.

Hake rarely accepts consignments, preferring to own the material that he auctions. Hake's Americana & Collectibles mail auctions are excellent for middle-market and low-end material, especially toys, games, and puzzles manufactured after 1920. Whether you participate or not, the catalogs are an important resource for determining what is available in the market.

- New England Auction Gallery, P.O. Box 8087, East Lynn, MA 01904.

Debby and Mary Krim, owners of the New England Auction Gallery, became a major factor in the mail order auction sector in the 1980s. A typical sale consists of between 350 and 400 lots. They place special emphasis on securing toys in the upper condition grades and with their original boxes. All items have a reserve that is clearly noted. Results from the previous sale accompany each catalog.

The bulk of the lots offered for sale date from the post-World War II period. They reflect what is hot and trendy in the toy market. Recently, sales have been very strong on battery operated, friction, and windup toys manufactured in lithographed tin.

- Smith House Toy Sales, 26 Adlington Rd., Eliot, ME 03903.

Smith uses the same approach as the New England Auction Gallery. Four auctions are held each year, featuring between 350 and 400 lots each; material is largely post-1945. Two features differentiate Smith's catalog: it is printed in full color and contains condition reports for all boxes. Auction results are published and mailed separately.

Others

More and more dealers are using the mail auction technique to sell merchandise. They begin by running mini-auctions, listing the auction items in a full page advertisement in *Toy Shop* or one of the other trade papers. Bidding is done largely by telephone. Once they build up a client base, they start issuing catalogs. Among the firms or individuals that you might wish to contact are:

- Continental Auctions, P.O. Box 193, Sheboygan, WI 53082.
- Global Toy Merchants, Inc., Rex and Kathy Barrett, P.O. Box 254, Medinah, IL 60157.
- Historicana. Robert Culp, 1632 Robert Road, Lancaster, PA 17601.
- Joe Hylva, P.O. Box 176, Grapeville, PA 15634.
- Rex Stark, 49 Wethersfield Rd., Bellingham, MA 02019.

Toy Shows

Shows devoted exclusively to toys, games, and puzzles became a fixture in the 1980s, and the number is still growing. Dealers and collectors alike have become alarmed by this trend. They often spend two or three weekends each month attending specialized shows. In many cases, there is more than one show in a particular locality on the same weekend. Just how far dealers and merchandise can be spread is now one of the most-asked questions.

As a collector, you have three goals at every show you attend. First, you want to buy toys, games, or puzzles for your collection. Second, you want to make as many dealer contacts as possible. Finally, you want to identify and talk with other collectors. Remember, more toys, games, and puzzles are sold over the telephone and through the mail than at shows. Shows put people in touch with each other.

When attending a show, identify the dealers who sell the type of toy, game, or puzzle that you collect. Get their business cards and enter the information about them in your files. Double check to make certain the card contains a full mailing address and the telephone area code. You will be surprised how many do not. Every other month you should phone a dozen key dealers with whom

Fig. 4-3 There are many specialized outdoor toy shows across the country.

you do business to see if they have acquired any material of interest to you. Keeping in contact is a two-way street.

Do not ignore the general dealers. Dealers often buy toys, games, and puzzles in lots. Once they have removed the toys, games, and puzzles that they like to sell, they often sell the balance to another dealer for a low price. You can interrupt that flow and get some great bargains if your interests do not coincide with the dealer's, and if you position yourself as the person to whom that dealer can turn for a quick and easy sale.

Use every chance to hand out your want list. All right, three-quarters of them will be thrown out. All you care about are the ones that bring results. Do not be afraid to hand them to other collectors, especially if their collecting interests differ. Collectors often tip off other collectors when their interests do not conflict.

Rather than attend a large number of shows, attend your favorite shows over and over again. Always sample a few new shows each year, but remember that the old reliables produce the best hunting. First, because dealers fight for the same spot each time so that repeat customers can find them easily, you will know exactly where to go. Second, dealers often contact their regular customers prior to a show to let them know if they are bringing material of interest. In many cases, they will offer to hold an item until you arrive. Third, socializing is a very important part of the buying process. Attending a show where you know the layout allows time for this nicety.

Specialized toy, game, and puzzle shows now number in the hundreds. Many do not occur on a fixed schedule. To locate them, start by checking the show advertising in the periodicals. At the shows you do attend, there will be a table with cards and broadsides advertising upcoming shows. Pick up one of each so that you can study them later. As you meet dealers and collectors, ask them which shows they do, and ask them to evaluate the show.

The following list reflects the diversity of shows and show promoters. It is only designed to get you started on the show circuit. Shows are listed al-

Fig. 4-4 Indoor shows offer the opportunity to buy toys year-round. Some are highly specialized, such as the East Coast Toy Soldier Show and Sale.

Fig. 4-5 Indoor shows provide an excellent opportunity for collectors and dealers to meet and exchange information.

phabetically by the city in which they appear. In no way should the list be considered a ranking of importance.

- Allentown, PA: Allentown Toy Show. Allentown Fairgrounds, first Saturday in November; D. K. Bausch, promoter.
- Austin, TX: Austin Collectors Exposition. March and November; Bill Wallace, promoter.
- Boston, MA: Northeast Collectibles Extravaganza. Bayside Expo Center, first weekend in December; Show Promotions, Inc., promoter.
- Glendale, CA: The All-American Collector's Show. Glendale Civic Auditorium, third weekend in January.
- Lyndhurst, NJ: The Meadowlands Classic Television And Toy Convention. Quality Inn, third Saturday in August; G.A. Corp., promoter.
- Macungie, PA: Das Awkscht Fescht Toy Show, Eyer Jr. High School, first weekend in August; D. K., Bausch promoter.
- Maumee, OH: Toledo Collectors' Toy Fair, Lucas County Recreation Center, second Sunday in March, July, and October; John Carlisle, promoter.
- Miami, FL: Miami Antique Toy Show, Hotel Sofitel, first Sunday in February; Tom Graboski and Steve Fuller, promoters.
- Nashville, TN: Nashville Antique Toy Show, Ramada Inn across from Opryland, second Saturday in May and November; Barry Gilmore, promoter.
- New York, NY: Kennedy International Antique Toy Convention, Viscount International Hotel at JFK, third Sunday in September; Bob Bostoff, promoter.
- Pasadena, CA: Toy & Collectibles Show and Sale, Pasadena Exhibit Center, first weekend in January and June; Doug Wright Productions, promoter.
- Phoenix, AZ: Arizona Toy Round-up, State

Fairground, first weekend in February; James and Rebecca Harscher, promoters.

- Raleigh, NC: The North State Toy & Hobby Show, North Carolina State Fairgrounds, second weekend in July; Carolina Hobby Expo, promoter.
- St. Charles, IL: Antique Toy & Doll World Show, Kane County Fairgrounds, third Sunday in April, June and October; Antique World Shows, Inc., promoter.
- St. Louis, MO: St. Louis Toy Show, Machinist Hall (12365 St. Charles Rock Road), fourth Sunday in September; John Tarrant, promoter.
- St. Paul, MN: Northland Antique Toy Show, Minnesota State Fairgrounds, first Sunday in May; Northland Toys Shows, promoter.
- San Mateo, CA: San Francisco International Antique Toy Show, San Mateo County Fairgrounds, fourth Sunday in August; Ron Hill and Jim Dugger, promoters.
- West Los Angeles, CA: West Los Angeles Antique Toy Show, Masonic Lodge, third Sunday of every month; The Attic Fanatic, promoter.
- York, PA: Greater York Toy, Doll & Holiday Show, York Fairgrounds, third Saturday in February; Jim Burke, promoter.
- Atlantique City, Atlantic City (NJ) Convention Center, third weekend in March; Brimfield Associates, Inc., promoter.

It hardly seems fair to single out one show above all others, but Atlantique City has become the largest and most important toy show in the United States. Dealers buy merchandise with Atlantique City in mind. Many pride themselves on exhibiting a booth that features entirely fresh merchandise, material they have never shown previously. The show features the broadest representation of American and foreign dealers.

The promoter claims that the show has more than 15 miles of aisles. It is so big that you simply cannot get through it in a day. The show attracts all levels of dealers. Prices for the same object vary considerably. Atlantique City is a mecca for the toy, game, and puzzle collector much as Brimfield is for the flea market circuit. You have to make the pilgrimage sooner or later if you are a devotee.

Fig. 4-6 Atlantique City, held each March at the Atlantic City Convention Center.

Buying Hints

The first step to buying successfully is to formulate a collecting philosophy. Force yourself to put it in writing. Having clear goals will prevent you from getting sidetracked, which can easily happen when you are collecting toys, games, or puzzles. After you have defined the purpose and scope of your collection, make a "wish list" of the items you would like to have. Prioritize the items and begin the hunt.

Since the vast majority of toys, games, and puzzles are sold via telephone or letter, develop a want list that you can send to dealers and collectors and hand out at flea markets, malls, shows, and shops. In addition to your list of toys, games, and

Fig. 4-7 Atlantique City, Second Exhibition Hall.

puzzles, your want list should contain the following basic information: your name, address, day and night phone numbers, conditions under which you buy, and the date. If you use a post office box for an address, provide a shipping address that includes a street number. Many dealers ship via UPS or similar carriers that cannot deliver to a post office box. Some collectors include an amount they are willing to pay for items, then grouse when everything is offered to them at that price or above. Let the seller quote; it is the seller's responsibility to set the price.

Make your want list as specific as possible. Dealers usually will not respond to a broadly worded request because they find that their quotes are refused more often than accepted. The fastest way to get a response is to assure the seller that a sale will be made if the price is right. Consider the following want list advertisement for mystery jigsaw puzzles:

Mystery Puzzles: read a book or pamphlet and put the puzzle together to get the clues to solve the crime. Key companies: Einson-Freeman (Mystery-Jig Puzzle, "Crime Club" series—three titles; "Problem" series—three titles), Jaymar (Detective Mystery Jigsaw Puzzle), Pearl Publishing Company (Mystery Puzzle of the Month—at least four known), and World Syndicate Publishing Co. (Mystic Jig).

Compare the advertisement with the following:

I am seeking the following mystery puzzles. Please quote only if the puzzle is complete, has a bright surface, all inserts (storybook) are present and the original box is in very good or better condition with no damage to top surface of the box.

NO QUOTES ON: American Publishing's Columbo Mystery Puzzle Game or Murder, She Wrote Mystery Puzzles; BePuzzled (all titles); International Polygonics, Ltd. (all titles); Jaymar Specialty's Detective Mystery Jigsaw Puzzle (Case of The Duke's Debtor); Pearl Publishing Company's Mystery Puzzle of the Month (unless No. 5 or higher). SEND QUOTES ON: Einson-Freeman Lithography Company: 1933 Crime Club series (CC-2 "The Torch Murder" and CC-3 "The 'Ringer's Revenge'"), 1933 Mystery-Jig series (No. 1 "The Matinee Murder" and No. 3 "Murder by the Stars"), 1933 Problem Jig-Saw series (PP-1 "Princess & Peasant" and PP-2 "The Jockey"). Story Puzzle Company: 1933 No. 1 "Five Finger Mark" (and any above).

The first listing appears detailed, but is not. A dealer's first reaction is that the collector probably has some of these puzzles or else he would not be able to come up with the list. It does not take a dealer long to learn that most collectors only want one of something and will seldom pay for a duplicate what was paid for their first one. While the

RINKER ENTERPRISES, INC.

P. O. Box 248
Zionsville, PA 18092

Day: (215) 966-3939
Night: (215) 966-5544

JIGSAW PUZZLE WANTS (September 1990)

I am a major collector of jigsaw puzzles, i.e., puzzles that make up into a picture. Listed below, in order of my collecting preference, are the specific categories of jigsaw puzzles that I collect and my wants within each category.

I rely heavily on individuals such as you to find the jigsaw puzzles that constitute my collection. I prefer to devote my energies to researching and writing about antiques and collectibles.

I welcome quotes. Better yet, phone. Over half my purchases are made via telephone.

Advertising puzzles

Buy a product or send in a box top or two and get a puzzle (either in a box or envelope). Advertising puzzles come in two types - puzzles that feature the product on the puzzle and those with product advertising only on the envelope or box. A major craze took place in the 1932-34 period, but some puzzles date as early as 1880 while others are contemporary. I buy all types and time periods.

No quotes on: ANGELUS/CAMPFIRE MARSHMALLOWS, CHASE AND SANBORN, COCOMALT, DIF (the Different Cleaner), KELLOGG'S, or LUX.

Mystery puzzles

Read a book or pamphlet and put the puzzle together to get the clues to solve the crime. Key series that I am seeking are: Einson- Freeman (Mystery-Jig Puzzle - four titles, "Crime Club" series - three titles, "Problem" series - four titles), Janus Games (four adult and three children's mysteries), Read Printing Co. (Detective Jig), Story Puzzle Company (Weekly Mystery Story Puzzle), Vitaplay Toy Company (Museum Mystery Jig Saw Puzzle), and World Syndicate Publishing Co. (Mystic Jig). If puzzle not listed above or below, quotes especially welcomed.

No quotes on puzzles by: AMERICAN PUBLISHING COMPANY, BEPUZZLED, INTERNATIONAL POLYGONICS LTD., JAYMAR SPECIALTY'S DETECTIVE MYSTERY JIGSAW PUZZLE (Case of Duke's Debtor); PEARL PUBLISHING COMPANY, and SPRINGBOK.

World War II puzzles

Any puzzle issued during World War II showing a battle scene, military aircraft, or other military subject.

Personality and Character puzzles

I prefer puzzles that show real people (movie stars, political figures, etc.). My cut off date is 1960, thus allowing me to include some of

Fig. 4-8 A general wants list.

RINKER ENTERPRISES, INC.

P. O. Box 248
Zionsville, PA 18092

Day: (215) 966-3939
Night: (215) 966-5544

DEPRESSION ERA WEEKLY PUZZLES (1932-33) WANT LIST AS OF 11/15/90

I am seeking the following weekly puzzles. Please quote only if the puzzle is complete, has a bright surface, all handouts are present, and the original box is in very good or better condition with no damage to the top surface of the box.

CROSS JIG PUZZLE (Commanday-Roth Co.)

Quote all titles

EVERY WEEK JIG-SAW PUZZLE (Einson-Freeman Co.)

11. Sea Horse
12. Peter Pan
14. The Challenge
21. Indians Hunting Buffalo
22. The First Lesson
23. The Warrior Prince
24. Sails and Seagulls
25. Menace of the Air
26. The Young Aviator
27. The Cradle Maker
28. Proud Parent
29. Prince of Dreams
30. In Conference
31. A Tough Spot
32. The Flower Peddler
33. Young Jig-Saw Makers
34. The Tease

JIG-OF-THE-WEEK (University Distributing Company)

[NOTE: Jig-of-the-Week puzzles were issued in four different border cuts. Quote all numbers (titles) with a non-straight edge border.]

1. No Title (American Sailing Ship)
2. Deauville Races 1932
3. Boat Race
4. The Prairie Fire
5. King Arthur's Country
6. Little Birds of the Shore
8. Thanksgiving
9. Buffalo Hunt

Fig. 4-9 A specific wants list.

dealer might drop a note about puzzles in stock, he is not likely to keep his eyes open and contact the collector when he finds an example in the field.

A dealer will pay attention to the second listing. It tells him exactly what the collector wants. It also tells him the collector is serious. You assist the dealer by placing a date on your want list. Dealers consider a list more than a year old as stale.

Trying to keep track of the individuals to whom you have distributed your want list is next to impossible, but try anyway. Each time you revise your list, send everyone a copy. It is a cheap reminder that you are still on the hunt. The persistent request does get answered.

Successful dealers keep good customer lists. Successful collectors keep good dealer lists. Go through the periodicals and trade papers and make a list of the toy, game, and puzzle dealers who sell the type of toy you collect. Put the information on index cards. Better yet, if you have a computer, use an inexpensive mailing program. Record mailing date and number of purchases.

Be realistic when selecting dealers that you plan to contact. Their advertisements provide more than enough information to recognize the level at which they price their merchandise. Contact only those dealers whose merchandise you can afford.

Make a dealer list and take it with you in the field. Make it a point to visit those dealers who have shops. Seek them out at toy shows. Introduce yourself and briefly explain your collecting interest. Carefully suggest your buying ranges. Of course, do not forget to give them a copy of your want list.

The good collector constantly cultivates sources. In order to have all the buying bases covered, there are two additional sources that need to be considered: direct-sale catalogs and lists, and classified advertising. The most important are direct-sale lists and catalogs.

Once a dealer has a strong customer list, he often publishes a direct-sale catalog. This is standard practice in the toy, game, and puzzle field. Among the better-known direct-sale operations are Just Kids Nostalgia (5 Green St., Huntingdon, NY 11743) and Toys Scouts, Inc. (330 Merriman Rd., Akron, OH 44303).

Some dealers charge for their catalogs. Catalogs can serve as important sources of pricing information and often cost more to produce than the amount requested, so paying to receive them is more than justified.

Other dealers use typed or computer-generated lists that are duplicated on photocopy machines, ranging in size from four to more than 20 pages. Lists are sent out when a dealer feels enough stock is on hand to justify a list. Previous buyers usually receive the list for free; others must send a self-addressed, stamped envelope and/or a fee of $1 to $2. Dealers often will sell merchandise on the list prior to mailing it. If you buy regularly from such a dealer, you may want to phone him every two or three months just to inquire what he may have added to his upcoming list.

Classified advertisements are a buying source that should be saved for last because of the enormous amount of time required to go through them and the modest results they produce. Enough periodicals are published in the antiques and collectibles field that you could spend the rest of your life reading the classifieds.

The biggest readers of classified advertisements are dealers, not collectors. You should try to make them your eyes as well by organizing a viable want list and distributing it widely. Of course, you are going to pay a premium for an item because the dealer found it, not you. Who cares? Multiply the value of your time by the hours that you would spend combing the classified advertising without results. The premium that you pay a dealer to do it for you is money very well spent.

Trading Toys, Games, and Puzzles

Trading is common among toy, game, and puzzle collectors. As with all other aspects of collecting, there are no fixed rules. This makes many collectors uncomfortable. Some become so uncomfortable that they absolutely refuse to become involved in trading. You have to decide what is right for you.

One of the difficulties with trading is that it has been turned into a competitive game. The winner is the person who gets the best deal and bragging rights. Never underestimate the power of bragging rights in the toy, game, and puzzle field.

The key to trading toys, games, and puzzles is to develop apples-to-apples comparisons. A great deal of trading takes place without value being mentioned. This is ridiculous—value is the one constant measure. The smart trader trades value for value. If seller and buyer agree to the market value of the objects involved in the trade, add up the values, and balance the equation with cash, then both sides get equal value. There is no winner or loser. If it were only this simple!

Dealers have a strong tendency to value everything they want to acquire at wholesale prices and everything they want to trade at retail. Do not allow it. Insist on retail value for trading purposes. If the balance paid in cash goes to you, you will receive far more than if you traded at wholesale value. Of course, this method works against you if it is you who must make up the difference in cash. A good trade involves a minimal amount of cash.

Dealers are pussycats compared to collectors. Getting two collectors to agree on a toy's worth is next to impossible. Collectors almost always have an inflated view of the condition and worth of the material in their collections, especially when they are trading. Further, they have very fixed ideas of the value (universally, much lower than the market value) of the item for which they wish to trade. Collectors may not mind paying the higher price to a dealer, but they resent using that price as a gauge in the trading process.

Most collectors trade duplicates. Before trading any item, carefully compare it to the one you plan to keep. Is it exactly the same? Collectors place great value on variations. If there are noticeable differences, keep both objects. For example, Pepsodent's "The Goldbergs" die-cut advertising jigsaw puzzle from the early 1930s was cut with two different dies. While some collectors might be content merely to own an example of the puzzle, a serious advertising puzzle collector wants both die-cut versions represented in his collection.

Condition is another key element to consider. Often the comparison is not clear. The surface of one toy might be bright but have a few flaws, while the surface of a second toy is dull but without flaws. Which toy do you keep? The answer is simple: both of them.

Once you have identified trade material, make a list. At the top of the first page, state the terms and conditions under which you are willing to trade. Stick to them. Make your listing as detailed as possible. Be objective about condition. Indicate your opinion of market value. Also list some of the items that you are seeking.

Those who have been collecting for less than two years should not even consider trading. You need two years to get a good grasp of pricing, a clear recognition of which pieces are common and which are rare, and enough contacts with other collectors and dealers to make trading possible. Trading should never be used as a substitute for buying an item outright.

Buying duplicate material solely for trading is not recommended unless the toy, game, or puzzle is in the hard-to-find or masterpiece category and you can buy it at one-quarter to one-third its market value. Do not tie up your money in something of little value to you. It is far better to spend your money on items not yet in your collection. Never lose sight of the fact that your most important objective is to build *your* collection, not someone else's.

One of the hardest things not to consider during the trading process is what you paid for the object. If you follow the principles above, your trading stock will have been purchased at bargain prices. You have no obligation to pass these bargains on to someone else. The only price that counts in a trade is the market value that you are using as a base.

Before you trade those duplicates, think about having an historical society, museum, college, university, or library sponsor an exhibit of your collection. This means that part of your collection will be absent from your home for an extended period of time. Because some risk is involved in lending material, collectors use duplicate collections for lending purposes. The best examples never leave home.

A few collectors—rare exceptions—use duplicates as gifts or sell them very inexpensively to a beginning collector. If you are a gift giver, do not keep score. Give without the expectation of return. It is your choice, not the receiver's. Helping a new collector begin qualifies you for sainthood. The key to the survival of the toy, game, and puzzle market is new collectors.

Finally, if trading makes you uncomfortable, don't do it. Do not allow anyone to force you to do it. Trading is mentally exhausting. Only you know if you would be better off channeling these energies to another aspect of your collection.

Selling Toys, Games, and Puzzles

There are many reasons for collectors to become sellers. They may have acquired similar pieces in better condition, acquired unwanted material in a large lot, changed collecting emphasis, or simple need funds to buy a highly desired piece. The list is endless. Because of their attachment to their pieces, selling generally starts with only a few pieces at a time.

Collector, Dealer, or Both?

Once you decide to sell, an important decision has to be made: Will you sell regularly or occasionally? If the answer is regularly, you must become a dealer. This means applying for a sales tax number, keeping a separate business account, and filing the necessary tax reports. You should consult with your accountant and attorney to see what advantages this route has to offer. If you are only going to sell occasionally, you probably will conduct your business ''under the table.'' If you do not report your profits for tax purposes, you are in violation of state and federal laws. The fact that everyone does it does not make it right.

If you decide to become a collector/dealer, be prepared for animosity from time to time. Collectors get angry because you keep the best pieces for yourself rather than sell them. Dealers get angry because you are cutting into their profits and operating outside the traditional roles. To explore the options available in dealing toys, games, and puzzles, consult the following books:

- Baker, Robert M. *How to Become a Weekend Antiques Dealer for Fun & Profit.* Niles, Mi: Acorn Press (P.O. Box 32, Niles, MI 49120), 1980.
- Barlow, Ronald S. *How to be Successful in the Antiques Business, Revised Edition.* New York: Charles Scribner's Sons, 1981.
- Johnson, Bruce E. *How to Make $20,000 a Year in Antiques & Collectibles without Leaving Your Job.* New York: Rawson Associates, 1986.
- Miner, Robert G. *The Flea Market Handbook, Second Edition.* Radnor, Pa: Wallace-Homestead, 1990.

Selling a Few Objects

If you are only going to sell a few objects, offer them first to other collectors. Whenever you visit other collectors and see something that you covet, never hesitate to say, ''When you want to sell that, call me.'' You will be surprised how many will remember. Similarly, when someone makes the same comments viewing your collection, jot down his name.

If you are selling core and above-average pieces, consider contacting a beginning collector you have met through a collectors' club or who has approached you. Nothing helps promote your field more than encouraging new collectors. If you are selling a piece an advanced collector needs, contact him.

Every collector wants to sell his toys, games, and puzzles for top dollar. This approach is not practical. If a buyer wants to pay top dollar, he will buy the toy from a dealer. When selling to a collector, expect to realize between 70 and 80 percent of market price; the scarcer the object, the higher the percentage.

If you decide to approach a dealer, first offer the toy to the dealer from whom you purchased it. Many dealers are delighted to reacquire objects that they have sold. When selling to a dealer, you can expect to receive 40 to 60 percent of current market value; the greater the value, the higher the percentage. Forget what you paid for it. What counts is its present market value.

Your final approach is to place an advertisement in a trade periodical. If you are selling commonly found items at a substantial discount from current market prices, this approach works very well. Classified advertising rates range from 10 to 30 cents a word, making them a true advertising bargain.

You will achieve the most success with classified advertising when your wording combines preciseness with conciseness. Fortunately, most toys, games, and puzzles can be described in 10 words or less because they are so well known among collectors. Always include a note about completeness, condition, and availability of original box. Provide your telephone number. Classified buyers are used to contacting sellers immediately to be sure they have the object. A promise to send a check is one thing, the actual check is another. When selling through the classifieds, it pays to make a waiting list for the toy in case the initial buyer fails to honor his commitment.

When selling through classified ads, always insist on payment before you ship the object. The preferred method of payment is check or money order. In most cases you will not know the person on the receiving end, so many collectors wait until the check or money order actually clears before shipping. Package the toy carefully and insure it. Many carriers, such as UPS, are reluctant to insure antiques and collectibles. The United States Postal Service has no such reservations.

Selling Your Collection

It is the rare collector who never sells in the course of collecting. As your collection grows, you have the responsibility for its future. If you are going to pass it on, do so with a warm hand rather than a cold one. There are many options. You might make it a planned part of your estate, donate it to a museum, or take the money and run. It is time to consider the latter.

You need a sales plan to successfully sell a collection. Toys, games, and puzzles, unless in the hard-to-find or masterpiece category, are difficult to liquidate quickly. In many cases, the right sales plan involves a variety of approaches. Taking time to develop a plan forces you to consider all the options.

Decide how much of a market manipulator you want to be. There are numerous ways to stimulate interest in a subject. If you do decide to manipulate the market, be careful not to allow the manipulation to be traced directly to you. The manipulators of the 1980s have left a bitter trail across the entire antiques and collectibles field, not just the toy sector. To better understand the possibilities and pitfalls, read my book, *How to Make the Most of Your Investments in Antiques and Collectibles* (Arbor House, 1988).

Timing is critical. If you are conservative, sell in a stable market. If you have spent several decades building up your collection, the returns are not likely to disappoint you. A common adage among collectors is, "Wait long enough and even your mistakes turn a profit." Of course, the ideal time to sell is when your portion of the market is running hot.

Consider testing the waters. Sell a few items to

see how the market reacts. Use some core and above-average items for the testing. Masterpiece and hard-to-find objects are not good tests because they do well regardless of the general state of the market. If the test items do not realize the prices that you expect, reconsider your sales plan.

There are many sale options: public auction, absentee auction, consignment, sales list, tag sale, or private sale (either as a collection or individually) to a collector, dealer, or museum. All have advantages and disadvantages. Explore each technique carefully. Consider a combination of approaches. Do not allow anyone to force you to choose before you are ready.

Because selling a collection is such an intensely personal experience, it may be best to turn the process over to someone else. If you select the auction route, do not attend. You will leave heartbroken, haunted by the memory of all the pieces that did not realize what you thought they should, and totally forgetting the pieces that sold way above estimate. However, before you turn your collection over to anyone, make certain you have a contract that clearly defines the rights and obligations of both parties.

Once you have determined the approach, proceed full-steam ahead. Do not look back; you have made up your mind. Walk away. Easy advice to givc, but difficult to follow. But thc moncy you receive for your collection will open up new opportunities. If you are like most collectors, it will probably mean a new collecting adventure in another category.

CHAPTER 5

Is What I Have Genuine?

Every collector lives with the fear of being fooled by a reissue, reproduction, copycat, fake, or fantasy item—and with good reason. They are rampant in the toy sector and exist to a lesser extent in the game and puzzle sector. But this does not mean that you should give up in despair and simply not collect.

Simply knowing that reissues, reproductions, copycats, fakes, and fantasy items exist puts you on guard. If you follow a few common sense rules, you will avoid most of the pitfalls. Experience provides the remaining skills that allow you to avoid the problem altogether.

Reissues, Reproductions, Copycats and Fakes

What exactly is the difference between a reissue, reproduction, copycat, fake, and fantasy item? Once you know, spotting them becomes much easier.

A reissue is a new toy, game, or puzzle made using the original molds, dies, or printing plates. All too often collectors forget to ask the basic question, "What happened to the original molds?" The assumption is that they were destroyed, but that is not necessarily true. The molds used to cast Hubley and Grey Iron products today belong to Dansco, parent company of John Wright Company, Wrightsville, PA. They were acquired when Dansco purchased the Grey Iron Company. John Wright continues to make castings from them. Original toy molds, dies, and printing plates surface in the marketplace from time to time and are eagerly purchased by dealers and collectors. Some mold owners offer legitimate reissues on a limited edition basis. An unscrupulous few use them to make new castings that they pass as originals.

A reproduction is an exact copy of an original piece. The manufacturing process used to make it may differ significantly from that used to make the original. The intent is to duplicate the original as closely as possible. In the case of toys, this often means taking an old toy, breaking it down into its component parts, making new molds and dies, and remanufacturing the piece. The final product is not an exact duplicate. There are subtle differences the advanced collector can detect to differentiate between the reproduction and the original.

A key point to make about reproduction toys, games, and puzzles is that they generally start out life honestly—that is, they are sold as reproductions. Most reproductions are marked or labeled. But remove the marking or label, add some artificial aging, and the reproduction can often be passed as an original.

A copycat is a stylistic copy of an object, not an exact copy. Often it represents an entirely new form or design. There are enough similarities, however, that someone unfamiliar with the original may confuse it with the original.

When a copycat is made during the original period of a toy, game, or puzzle's production, it is called a "knock-off." Manufacturers are diligent in their efforts to ferret out these unlicensed products. The collector takes a slightly different attitude: often, because of their scarcity, unlicensed products are eagerly sought for collections.

In the case of toys, games, and puzzles, a copycat might also be a product that imitates another in format, theme, or style, but not in name. For example, an entire collection could be made of Monopoly copycats. True, each game might be unique and, therefore, "original," but only a fool would fail to see the similarity.

A fake is an object that is deliberately meant to deceive. The maker often uses the same tools and techniques that the original manufacturer used. The faker's principal contribution is adding aging characteristics so as to prevent differentiating between the modern fake and the period example.

Fakes often are one-of-a-kind, while reproductions and copycats generally are mass-produced. As a result, it is possible to keep track of reproductions and copycats and to tell others how to distinguish them from the originals. It is much more difficult with fakes.

Fantasy items are objects manufactured after the death (e.g., Elvis), break-up (e.g., the Beatles), or revival (e.g., Star Trek) of a person or group. Many of these items take a highly romanticized and emotional approach. There are two motivations for fantasy items: idealism and greed. The idealist sees the fantasy item as a memorial, something that says, "I'll never forget you" or, "You'll always be in my heart." These are the toy, game, and puzzle fanatics that are fans, devotees, and worshippers. The same sentiments do not motivate most manufacturers. Their principal motivation seems to be capitalizing on a good thing as long as it lasts.

Fantasy items often lack quality. Many are cheap and junky. The 1989 Batman ideas do not meet the standards set by the early 1970s Batman products. Dick Tracy collectors will acquire the 1990 Dick Tracy licensed products because they are part of the story. It rarely occurs to the collector to compare them with their historic counterparts in respect to design, faithful adherence to the character, and manufacturing quality. If they did, they would shy away from these later products. Never forget, the highest value always rests with the toys, games, and puzzles that were licensed and manufactured during the early period. I hope it will never change.

The term "fantasy" is sometimes used to thinly disguise an outright fake. The Hopalong Cassidy guitar that comes in a Jefferson Toy Company box was never manufactured during the original period of Hopalong Cassidy toys, nor was it licensed by the individuals who now control the rights to the Hopalong Cassidy character. Its quality is of the poorest kind. Yet, this piece sells in the $50 to $100 range. Why? Because all too often collectors lose the ability to discriminate. Don't fall into this trap.

While poor quality may distinguish many fantasy items, it is a mistake to assume that reproductions, copycats, and fakes are poorly made. The John Wright Company's mechanical bank reproductions are of excellent quality and design, and differ significantly from the cheap reproduction made in Asia.

Some claim that every new toy, game, and puzzle is nothing more than a redesigned toy, game, or puzzle from the past. There is more truth in this statement than is apparent. As toy, game, and puzzle collecting reached record peaks in the 1980s, manufacturers saw a new market developing for their products: collectors themselves. There are now toy, game, and puzzle lines specifically for collectors.

The three toy areas where this phenomenon is most noticeable are trains, soldiers, and vehicles. Companies such as Eccles Brothers of Burlington, IA are using original Barclay, Manoil, and other old molds to make new castings. Technically, these are reissues. However, Wayne and Mary Hill of New Hampshire have created entirely new designs in the dime store soldier tradition. It is not fair to call these copycats or fantasy items. They are simply new toys. The difference may appear subtle, but it is not to a toy, game, or puzzle collector. The good news regarding these new toys is that they are often of the highest quality, and manufacturers take care to mark them properly so they cannot be confused with their historical counterparts.

Ten Commonsense Rules

When a toy, game, or puzzle category becomes "hot," reissues, reproductions, copycats, and fakes generally follow close behind. The wise collector must become a detective. In a business where *caveat emptor* ("let the buyer beware") is the general rule, it is up to the collector to develop the skills that allow him to collect without fear. The task is not as difficult as it may seem. All one has to do is follow 10 simple rules.

It does not take sophisticated equipment to spot most reissues, reproductions, copycats, fakes, and fantasy items. It only takes common sense. Look at toys, games, and puzzles with your head, not your heart; save the love affair until after you have bought your prize.

▪ ***Rule 1: If it looks new, assume it is new.***

Toys, games, and puzzles were meant to be used. They should have signs of age and use. This is one of the most important reasons for always asking how a toy, game, or puzzle was played with. When you know the method of play, you know the places you should expect to see wear. Every mark should have a logical reason for being there. When the proper wear marks are not present, be suspicious.

The toy, game, and puzzle field abounds with stories of items that were put away on the day they were acquired and never played with. However, storage itself produces deterioration. Boxes get dusty. Being stacked on top of one another, they often get misshapen. Painted surfaces mellow and sometimes crack, especially if the toy was stored in an attic or basement where it experienced temperature or humidity extremes. Minor but noticeable surface deterioration can occur on lithographed tin toys.

Look at yourself in the mirror: Do you look the same as you did ten years ago? Time takes its toll; an old toy, game, or puzzle should have signs of age.

Manufacturers of reproductions and copycats make little effort to artifically age their products. Restorers and fakers take the time to age and distress pieces, but only in the visible places. Rarely

Fig. 5-1 When handling a toy such as Lehmann's Masuyama Family, check its weight, pay close attention to paint color tones, look for signs of wear where they should be, and evaluate its aesthetics.

will the faker properly age a piece on the bottom or in the interior. Therefore, these regions provide the best clues for determining the actual age of an object.

- ***Rule 2: Handle 500 good examples in your collecting category, either at the home of a collector, the shop of a dealer, or a museum.***

There is no substitute for handling the real thing. Develop a sense for the proper feel of the object, its weight and surface texture. Note the detail, the color tones, and how it is made. Caress the object, stroke it gently, learn to recognize it in the dark. Once you have familiarized yourself with the genuine article, you will never have trouble spotting a reissue, reproduction, copycat, fake, or fantasy item.

Many museums and historical societies have toy, game, and puzzle study collections. The most famous is the Margaret Woodbury Strong Museum in Rochester, NY. The library at your local museum or historical society probably has a museum directory that will allow you to identify the toy, game, and puzzle collections nearest you. A letter to the curator explaining your interest and expressing a desire to visit and study the collection often leads to an invitation.

Auction previews are an excellent place to handle material. This is one reason it is more important to attend the preview than the sale. Select a number of items from the catalog and check your observations against those of the cataloger. Chances are that other collectors will be doing the same. If you see someone you recognize, work together and exchange views.

The best place to view toys, games, and puzzles is in a collector's or dealer's private collection. In many cases, this person is far more knowledgeable than the museum curator or auctioneer. A good collection may also include reissues, reproductions, copycats, fakes, and fantasy items. Encourage the collector to show you this part of the collection and to explain the differences.

- ***Rule 3: Examine toys, games, and puzzles in natural sunlight whenever possible.***

Fluorescent light has a strong tendency to change the color of objects, especially their paint tones. One of the hardest things for manufacturers to do is match colors. Sunlight allows the best color examination.

Many antiques malls, shops, and shows are poorly lit. If you ask the owners or promoters about this, they say they did the best they could. Do not believe it. Poor lighting helps cover up minor defects. Experienced collectors know this and guard against it.

If enough light is not available to examine an object properly, you must supplement it. The usual tool is a flashlight. When using a flashlight, rake the light over the surface. Do not shine the light directly on the toy, game, or puzzle, as the glare will continue to hide the very defects you are trying to discover.

- ***Rule 4: Examine all aspects and sides of a toy, game, or puzzle.***

Pick up the toy, game, or puzzle to examine it. Challenge yourself to let no surface, including interior surfaces, go unseen. Take your time. If you are in a sales environment, once you have an object in your hand, it is yours until you put it down.

If it is impossible to examine a toy, game, or puzzle adequately where it is displayed, ask the owner if you can move it to a location where a proper inspection can be made. Never buy an item that you have not handled. Your fingers tell you not only about the authenticity of an object, but a great deal about its condition as well.

If it comes apart, take it apart. Take it all apart. However, you must be prepared to put it back together. If you cannot, do not take it apart. Always ask the dealer's permission before taking anything apart. In fact, it might be wisest to ask the dealer to take apart the item for you.

▪ *Rule 5: Consistency is the key.*

All parts of every toy, game, or puzzle should be made the same way and exhibit the same quality of workmanship. If a toy has two or more sections, the construction techniques used to make one section should match those used to make the others. This is one of the quickest ways to detect a reconstructed part.

When examining period toys, games, and puzzles, it is extremely important to examine the finishing of the product. How carefully were the casting flanges removed from a cast iron toy? What care was used to apply the paint and other decoration? Note the tightness of the joints. The easiest way to spot reproduction cast iron toys is the lack of attention to finishing detail, resulting in rough edges to the castings and poorly fitting joints.

If the toy is symmetrical, mentally draw a line down the center and compare it section by section. Everything should match. If the toy is asymmetrical, make certain the pieces look like they belong together. Consistency also implies harmony of parts.

This is a good rule, but like all rules, it has exceptions. Check the famous Toonerville Trolley lithographed tin toy. The lithography on all the parts is excellent except for the conductor's hands. There is no lithography on them at all. When you first see an example of this toy, this inconsistency jumps out and may make you highly suspicious. However, a check of other surviving examples shows that, in this case, the inconsistency is the consistency.

▪ *Rule 6: The Lindquist Apology Theory.*

"If a person apologizes for a toy, game, or puzzle more than four or five times, or if you find four or five major things wrong with it, accept the inevitable conclusion that the object has been highly restored, reconstructed, or is an outright fake."

Although David Lindquist developed this rule for the inspection of antique furniture, it works equally well for toys, games, and puzzles. A questioning mind is not good enough. Learn to ask questions when you spot a problem. Be aggressive. Sometimes it even results in a lower price.

Many dealers have a ready answer for any question that you ask about a toy, game, or puzzle. A question that may seem novel to you probably has been heard many times by the dealer. Their answers are "tradecraft," and are passed from dealer to dealer. Some are:

"Of course it's damaged—it's old, isn't it?"

"I never noticed that. I don't think many others will, either."

"So the puzzle is missing a few pieces. You can have them replaced easily."

"You will have no trouble finding the missing parts."

These answers are nothing more than apologies. Accept them as such.

I am not implying that answers provided by dealers are not accurate. In many cases, they are plausible. A wise collector buys a toy, game, or puzzle that raises the fewest questions possible. Any questions are likely to be asked again by the person to whom you try to sell the piece. One hopes that you will remember the answers that you received and be extremely convincing as you pass them on.

▪ *Rule 7: Use a second set of eyes.*

There it is—the item for which you have been looking for years. Your eyes become glassy, you float over to the object of your affections, you pick it up gently—you have completely lost your objectivity. You need help; call in the shock troops.

Go shopping with a friend, preferably another collector, but one who does not collect what you collect, so as to ensure the total sincerity of his advice. Your friend is along to keep asking you two basic questions: Do you know what you are doing? You are going to spend *how much* for that?

- ***Rule 8: Beware of bargains.***

There are bargains left. However, if the price is low and the toy, game, or puzzle appears to be a real bargain, be doubly alert. Many reissues, reproductions, copycats, fakes, and fantasy items enter the market priced between 50 and 70 percent less than their historical counterparts. Dealers who try to pass these items as original want the collector to be convinced that he is pulling a fast one on the poor, ignorant dealer. With the wealth of literature and price guides available in the toy, game, and puzzle field, there is little reason to believe a dealer is ignorant.

Bargains do exist. When you find them, take advantage of them. Price is only a warning sign. When it is much lower than it should be, alarm bells should go off in your mind. If it is a false alarm, buy the item.

- ***Rule 9: Remember where and what you have seen in the past.***

If you see a great-looking toy, game, or puzzle that you have not seen before in your travels, and then see an identical example a few booths or shops later, you might be facing a reissue, reproduction, copycat, or fantasy item. Because reissues, reproductions, copycats, and fantasy items are mass produced, they come into the market in quantity.

Force yourself to memorize every reproduction, copycat, and fake known in your collecting specialty. This puts you on guard. It also educates you in how the material in your collecting field has been reproduced, copied, or faked, thus providing the criteria by which to judge new objects.

- ***Rule 10: Create a file on reissues, reproductions, copycats, fakes, and fantasy items.***

Identify the manufacturers and wholesalers who make and distribute these products. Write for their catalogs. Pay whatever it costs to acquire them; they will be invaluable reference sources in the future. If possible, actually visit the wholesalers' warehouses to view and handle the reissues, reproductions, and copycats. There is no substitute for hands-on experience.

In addition to manufacturers and wholesalers, also keep track of reproduction craftsmen and the gift shop trade. Do not make the mistake of assuming that all material originates inside the collecting field. Many craftsmen issue catalogs. Write for them. The next time you are in a large city, such as New York, Atlanta, or Dallas, visit the merchandise mart. Ask your local gift shop to save all their old catalogs for you.

Clip or photocopy all articles and notes that appear in trade magazines and newspapers about reissues, reproductions, copycats, fakes, and fantasy items. You will be surprised how much information you can find. A major source of information is collectors' clubs. Their newsletters, bulletins, and journals make a strong effort to pass along information to their members as quickly as it is known.

Invest in books. Although they do not deal specifically with toys, games, and puzzles, Dorothy Hammond's *Confusing Collectibles: A Guide to Identification of Contemporary Objects* (Des Moines, IA: Wallace-Homestead, 1979) and Ruth Webb Lee's *Antiques, Fakes & Reproductions* (Wellesley Hills, MA: 1950) are well worth owning. Their values rests in showing how widespread the reissue, reproduction, and copycat problem is. Unfortunately, both books are out of print. Lee's book went through seven editions; if you can find it, buy the fourth or later editions, not the first three.

- ***The Unwritten Rule: Share your knowledge and spread the word.***

It is time collectors entered into an era of cooperation in the toy, game, and puzzle field instead of perpetuating the old "trade secrets" mentality. Ignorance is not bliss, it is ignorance.

When you spot a reissue, reproduction, copycat, fake, or fantasy item being passed as a period original, make a note of where you saw it and

Fig. 5-2 A catalog page from Pride Lines Ltd.

how you identified it. Send this information to the trade papers and appropriate collectors' clubs. Tell your friends. Ask them to spread the word.

Spreading the word about such objects is not enough. Spread the word about the person doing the deceiving as well. The only police in the toy, game, and puzzle category are its participants; little help can be expected from outside authorities. No one likes to inform against another, but silence only condones bad practices.

A Final Analysis

At the moment, the problem of reissues, reproductions, copycats, fakes, and fantasy items is most prevalent in the toy area. More and more toy collectors are realizing the negative effect this material has and are working hard to make the information accessible to the public. This is an extremely positive sign.

Games and puzzles have been exempt from the problem largely because they have been relatively inexpensive and did not attract the attention of manufacturers of reissues, reproductions, and copycats. The situation is changing dramatically as prices for games and puzzles continue to rise.

Several games have celebrated their 50th anniversaries, and reproduction sets have been issued. In the 1970s, Milton Bradley reproduced a number of historic games and puzzles from its collection. Frame the reproduction Fire Department strip puzzle, and someone is going to be fooled.

Another threat is the color photocopy machine. It already is being used to duplicate boxes, which for many toys, games, and puzzles consist of a printed sheet pasted to cardboard. Color photocopying has reached a point where copies are difficult to distinguish except on close inspection. Missing game parts, instruction sheets, and pieces of puzzles also are being duplicated.

The problem does not rest with the replacement parts. Having them makes the game or puzzle more enjoyable, and even enhances the value somewhat. The problem rests with sellers who fail to reveal that some of the parts are not original. Whenever you replace a part, you have an obligation to make a note and place it with the object. Honesty *is* the best policy.

CHAPTER 6

Managing Your Collection

As a toy, game, and puzzle collector, you own a museum. What? You never thought of your collection this way? Well, you should. You are preserving and recording the past, displaying your collection for yourself and others to enjoy, and protecting it for future generations. This is exactly what a museum does.

You face the same problems that confront a small museum or historical society, many of which are run solely by volunteers. The American Association For State And Local History (AASLH), a national organization devoted to helping the small museum, is one of the best-kept secrets in the collecting field. Write to the AASLH (172 Second Ave., North, Nashville, TN 37201) and request a copy of their most recent book, videotape, technical leaflets, and reports catalog. There will be at least a dozen titles you will want to order immediately.

The AASLH technical leaflet series was begun in 1962 to provide brief, explicit, "how-to" information. Individual titles sell for $2 each. The following are just a few leaflets of interest to toy, game, and puzzle collectors: TL#10—Conservation of Metals; TL#11—Documenting Collections; Museum Registration and Records; TL#21—Methods of Research for the Amateur Historian; TL#31—Tax Problems of the Collector; TL#50—Insuring Against Loss; TL#83—Security for Museums and Historical Houses: An Annotated Bibliography; TL#88—Organizing Your 2 × 2 Slides: A Storage and Retrieval System; TL#91—Designing Your Exhibits: Seven Ways to Look at an Artifact; and TL#128—Effects of the Environment on Paper: A Review of Recent Literature. If you order any of these technical leaflets, mention that you read about them in this book so that the AASLH knows it enjoys broad-based support.

Creating a Record Catalog

Overall, toy, game, and puzzle collectors are very poor record keepers. They are so wrapped up in the acquisition of material that they never have time for cataloging. They pay lip service to it, faithfully promise themselves several times a year that they will do it, and die with the task unaccomplished.

You might put off cataloging, but what you cannot postpone is keeping an acquisition record—a list of the purchases that you make, filed chronologically. Actually, this is the first step toward cataloging. Museums maintain both an acquisition and a catalog file. Discipline yourself from the beginning to keep adequate acquisition records.

It helps to have a space in which to keep all new purchases until you complete an acquisition report. The only supplies you need are blank 8 × 10 sheets of paper, pencil, stapler, and a carpenter's rule. Your job will be greatly simplified if you get a sales receipt and business card (or at least name and address) from everyone from whom you purchase a toy, game, or puzzle.

Sales receipts are not as common in the toy, game, and puzzle sector as they are in other parts of the antiques and collectibles field, but they should be. A good sales receipt contains the name and full address of the person doing the selling, the date, a full description of the item purchased, the date the seller believes it was made, the amount paid, including the sales tax, and any guarantees under which the item was sold. The date of manufacture is critical; you may be able to prove fraud if you find that the toy, game, or puzzle was made several decades later. If you do not have a sales tax number, you pay sales tax. If the dealer does not collect it, that is one thing; refusing to pay it without a sales tax number is something very different.

Even though the sales receipt may have the seller's address and phone number, attempt to get a business card. Toy, game, and puzzle collectors and dealers often indicate their wants on their business cards. This is very helpful information. Again, check to see that the card includes the owner's name (a surprising number of cards only have the business name), full address (the street and zip code are frequently missing), and a phone number.

Upon returning home with your purchase, head for your acquisitions area. Staple the receipt and business card to the top of a sheet of paper. Make note of the date and place you purchased the object(s). When listing objects, provide a more complete description than on the sales receipt. Whenever possible, include measurements as part of that description. Make a note of the condition of the object and its box. If you bought a group of objects, you may want to reassign prices. Remember that the real worth of a toy, game, or puzzle is its value to you. Assign the individual items whatever prices you wish, just so the final total equals what you paid for the group. Finally, note how you paid for the object—with cash, check, or money order. File these sheets in chronological order. When you do find time to catalog your collection, these records will prove invaluable.

The acquisition record serves two additional purposes. First, they are often used as the basis for insurance coverage. Each sheet should be photocopied and stored in a location removed from the house or building that houses the original set. If there is a loss due to fire or theft, you have some protection.

Second, acquisition records are essential to the executor assigned to settle your estate. You would be surprised how few spouses, children, and executors known what a collector paid for his toys. Without this knowledge, one can easily be fleeced when disposing of a collection after the collector dies. No, you are not obligated to tell anyone the value of your collection during your lifetime, but do not leave them in the dark when you die. Of course, the downside of this practice may be revealed in cases of divorce, when acquisition records may haunt you.

Acquisition records are better than nothing, but they should never be viewed as a substitute for proper cataloging. Before doing any cataloging, read Daniel B. Reibel's *Registration Methods for the Small Museum*, published by the AASLH, and *Museum Registration Methods, Third Edition*, by Dorothy H. Dudley, Irma Bezold Wilkinson, et. al., published by the American Association of Museums in 1979. Reibel's book is currently out of print, but he is working on a revision that he plans to self-publish. Meanwhile, you will have to borrow a copy on inter-library loan or read it at your local museum or historical society.

The key to cataloging is to design a one-sheet form that contains all the basic information that you need. Do not bury yourself in paper work. Hold the cataloging information to one sheet. Once you have perfected your cataloging form, consider having it printed. If you have a computer, put the information into a data base. Unfortunately, the few software programs designed for cataloging antiques and collectibles do not work well for toys, games, and puzzles, which have unique information demands.

When you custom design your cataloging form, consider including most of the following information:

1. *Accession number and/or any other special numbers that you may assign to the object.* An accession number generally consists of a two-digit year number, a sequential number relating to purchases made that year, and a set number, if required. For example, 90.357.2 indicates the 357th item purchased in 1990, which contains at least two parts. You might want to allow additional space for a code for photographic negatives.
2. *Category name and subdivisions.* The main category is toy, game, or puzzle. Subdivisions might include manufacturer, object type, or time period.
3. *Title.* This is the formal title of the object—the name of the toy or game, the title of a puzzle.
4. *Description.* Describe the object in enough detail so that another collector might recognize it without a photograph. Provide as much detail as you can. In the case of a game, the description would include a listing of the playing pieces. List the number and configuration of pieces for a puzzle. Do not forget to include information about the box. Information about a distributor or licensing source should also be included in the description section.
5. *Maker and date of manufacture.* List the full name and address of the manufacturer. If the date of manufacture is unknown, list the copyright. If there is no copyright information, try to date the toy, game, or puzzle within a five-year period.
6. *Dimensions.* Round off to the nearest eighth of an inch. Use maximum width, depth, and height. Include additional measurements where appropriate. Provide a separate set of measurements for the packaging.
7. *Condition.* Grade the object. Using the codes explained earlier. Note all defects, including those that might have occurred in the making. If rebuilding, reconstruction, restoration, or conservation work was done, record it.
8. *Provenance.* This covers two key areas: a list of previous owners, and any places where this particular object was illustrated or exhibited. If the toy, game, or puzzle has an auction history, that also should be noted.
9. *Research.* Major research and pricing sources should be noted, and the results of research should be attached.
10. *Purchase information.* Include the full name and address of the seller, date of purchase, place of purchase, and amount paid. Do not forget to add the sales tax to the purchase price.
11. *Appraisal data.* It is important to understand the current value of your collection. The appraisal information should be updated every three to four years.
12. *Location.* This tells you where to find the object. Collectors do not spend a great deal of time rearranging their collections. Once an object is put somewhere, it tends to stay there. Location is usually indicated by room. If your toys, games, and puzzles are stored in boxes or files, they should be numbered and the appropriate number indicated.
13. *Comments.* This is the place for any information that you have that does not fit elsewhere on the form.
14. *Date the form was filled out or revised, and the initials of the person doing the cataloging.*

One additional thing you may want to consider is leaving space on your form for a small photograph of the object. The standard practice is to take 35mm black-and-white record photographs, have a contact sheet made of the negatives, and paste the individual shots on the catalog sheets. Make a note of the negative number so that if a larger picture is required, the negative can be located easily.

You also may have supporting documentation that you wish to file with the catalog sheet. This might be a copy of the acquisition sheet, photograph(s), conservation reports, articles or catalogs in which the object was illustrated, or research notes. Many collectors use a manila file folder for each object.

If you sell an object, consider passing along your catalog records to the new owner. There is no reason to make him repeat all the work that you have done. Likewise, if you purchase an object from a private individual, ask him to turn over any catalog records. If you purchase from a dealer, save your breath. They do not care about such records and are not about to reveal their sources of material to you.

Displaying Your Collection

Displaying toys is highly personal. The choices are endless. Some arrange by theme, others by size, color, manufacturer, or aesthetics. Current decorating styles stress the accent piece. Toys, games, and puzzles are a natural. Choose the display approach that gives you the greatest satisfaction. After all, they are your toys, games, or puzzles. The principal purpose of this section is to explore some of the dangers involved in displaying toys, games, and puzzles and what can be done to avoid them.

You hold your toys, games, and puzzles in trust. You have an obligation to care for them properly. Fulfilling this obligation means exposing them to as little harm as possible. It does not mean that you should worship them. Remember, toys, games, and puzzles are not much fun unless you can play with them. The solution is plenty of common sense and adult behavior.

The greatest threat to your toys, games, and puzzles is a rapid change in temperature. This can come from a variety of sources, such as exposure to sunlight, heating ducts, or outside walls. Excessive heat causes surface paint to crack, lithography to blister, and glue to lose adhesion. Never display toys, games, or puzzles above or in direct line with a heating or air conditioning duct. Check the heat generated by flood lighting. If you display toys, games, or puzzles in a lighted case, be concerned about the temperature buildup from the lights.

Under no circumstances allow any direct sunlight to strike your toys, games, or puzzles. Sunlight fades the colors. The differences may not be noticeable at first, but over time they become apparent, and there is virtually nothing that you can do to restore the original color. You also should be concerned if you use fluorescent, flood, or spot lighting to highlight your collection on a regular basis. These lights also can discolor surfaces. Protective devices that filter out harmful rays are available from a number of suppliers listed later in this chapter.

Toys, games, and puzzles often are displayed mounted on a wall, primarily on shelves. But walls with one face exposed to the exterior of the building ("outside" walls) may experience radical temperature shifts, and they may conduct heat or cold to the interior face. If you are going to use an outside wall for display, make certain there is plenty of airflow behind the objects. In addition, temperature is not always uniform in a room. Periodically check the areas where you display your toys, games, and puzzles to make sure that the temperature matches the general room temperature.

The second greatest danger to toys, games, and puzzles (particularly games and puzzles) is humidity. Rapid changes in humidity damage objects. The best environment is slightly on the humid side, about 55 to 60 percent. Unless your house is a completely closed environment, you have humidity problems. Purchasing a humidifier and dehumidifier—and using them properly—is a good investment.

Games and puzzle collectors need to be very concerned about silverfish, mites, and other insects that damage paper. Because of the large number of acquisition sources, every game and puzzle collector faces this problem sooner or later. It is a good policy to have your house fumigated on a regular basis. Learn to check each acquisition carefully before adding it to your collection. Are there any toy collectors chuckling? They probably have forgotten that their precious original boxes are subject to the same problems.

Keep your toys clean. It is not as simple as it sounds. If rubbed over the surface of a toy, game, or puzzle, dust will scratch it. The scratches are microscopic, but they are there. The ideal cleaning method is a light dusting with a feather duster. Some argue that this just moves the dust around, but it is better than using a vacuum cleaner brush and watching the paper cover of the box lid get sucked up with the dust.

Toys, games, and puzzles have to be cleaned individually. It should be done by someone with experience. In today's hectic world, many households employ cleaning help. These people are not collectors, and should be allowed to handle your toys, games, and puzzles only after proper training—and almost always under supervision.

Test the security of every surface on which you plan to place a toy, game, or puzzle. It should be able to support many times the weight that you are going to place on it. If the surface is slippery, you must make provisions to prevent the toy, game, or puzzle from falling off the front or sides. The simple act of walking can cause minor movement of surfaces within a room. A windstorm, blaring music, and a herd of teenagers are a few more examples of things that can send your toys, games, and puzzles into motion. Allow for minor disturbances when placing any toy, game, or puzzle on a shelf. If the object is close to the edge, it is not placed properly.

Not all toys, games, and puzzles are displayed on shelves. Some toys rest upon nails driven into the wall. Metal-to-metal contact is the result, and the danger of rust formation is strong. If a toy, game, or puzzle is going to rest on bars or be supported by a shelf stand, the points of contact should be padded with felt or some other soft material.

Never do anything that cannot be easily undone when preparing toys, games, or puzzles for display. For example, never, *never* glue puzzles to backing boards or cut the sides off game box lids in order to frame them. There are alternate ways, such as matting and shadow-box framing, to achieve the same end.

In short, apply common sense. Anticipate problems before they happen. Make the careful use of your toys, games, and puzzles a state of mind.

Storing Your Toys, Games, and Puzzles

The same considerations that govern the display of your toys, games, and puzzles also apply to their storage. Your principal concern is to prevent anything from damaging your collection. You must not become careless.

The first decision is how to store your toys, games, and puzzles. The standard method is in boxes, which are then stacked on top of one another. If you decide to pursue this method, make a commitment to using uniform boxes. The R-Kive Bankers Box or similar product is ideal. It does not have to be acid free if you wrap the toys, games, and puzzles that you place in the box in acid-free or chemically inert material.

Carefully wrap objects before placing them in a

box. Give careful thought to how well objects on the bottom will support the objects that will be placed on top of them. Pack each box loosely; forcing as many objects as possible into a box creates damage. Number and label each box. Make a list of what the box contains. Place one copy in the box, another in the storage area, and a third in your files.

While box storage is the norm, consider an alternative: sturdy industrial shelving. The concept is known as "open storage." The shelving is inexpensive and allows easier access to your toys, games, and puzzles, as well as free flow of air around the objects. Ensure protection of the toys, games, and puzzles that you store there by placing acid-free paper on the shelves so that the metal is covered. One way to keep dust out is to hang sheets down the sides of the shelves. When removing a toy, game, or puzzle, do not simply push the sheet out of the way. Either take if off or firmly secure it to one side.

A game collector used the upper shelf of his guest-room closet to store his games. When he took them down after several years, he found that the bottom boxes had been crushed. There is no way a game or puzzle collector can survive without storing boxes on top of one another. A few simple rules will help. First, never stack more than six boxes high. Second, stack largest to smallest, with the largest on the bottom. Third, ideally, cut a piece of acid-free (museum) mat board one inch larger on all sides than the box and place it on top of the box. Then place the next box on top of it and repeat the procedure until your stack is complete.

Once a year—more often if you live in a warm climate—have a pest-control expert check your storage area for pests. If any are found, take immediate action. However, make certain to discuss what chemicals and other forms of treatment the exterminator plans to use. If you are uncertain of the effect, call a conservation laboratory at a major museum (such as the Smithsonian or the Strong) to inquire if the treatment is harmful to your toys, games, and puzzles. If the answer is yes, you must explore other alternatives.

You do not find the supplies that you need to store toys, games, and puzzles in a hardware or department store. They come from special suppliers. The problem is that you rarely need large quantities. What are your alternatives?

First, contact the museums, historical societies, and libraries in your area and ask if you can arrange to purchase your supplies directly from their stock or combine your order with theirs. The latter procedure benefits both parties since quantity purchasers usually buy at a larger discount. Second, check your local artist's supply outlet. The art market has grown increasingly conservation-conscious during the past decade. Acid-free paper and mat board are often stock items. Third, if there is a conservation laboratory or independent conservator in your area, ask about direct or cooperative buying.

Several members of the The Ephemera Society of America sell archival supplies that pertain to the paper field. Write the society at P.O. Box 37, Schoharie, NY 12157, to get a list of names and addresses. These paper supplies are important when you consider all those boxes with broken corners that you have in your collection.

Other suppliers you may wish to contact are: Hollinger Corporation (P.O. Box 6185, Arlington, VA 22206) for folders, envelopes, storage boxes, document cases, and mylar sleeves; TALAS, a division of Technical Library Service, Inc. (130 Fifth Ave., New York, NY 10011) for storage boxes, and University Products, Inc. (P.O. Box 101, Holyoke, MA 11041) for a general line of supplies. *The Museum Archival Supply Handbook*, by the Ontario Museum Association and Toronto Area Archivist Groups, can be ordered from the AASLH. It lists more than 600 North American suppliers of archival materials. Many of the companies do not sell retail, but are glad to supply the name of the distributor nearest you.

Restoration and Conservation: Who Should Do It?

Sooner or later every collector is tempted to do some of his own restoration and conservation. Leave it to the professionals; you can do more harm than good. Often the best advice is not heeded, as is likely to happen in this case; proceed at your own risk.

If you are going to dabble, obtain a copy of A. Bruce MacLeish's *The Care of Antiques and Historical Collections*, another excellent publication from AASLH. The first eight chapters focus on establishing a conservation program. The next nine deal with the care and handling of objects according to composition. As a toy, game, or puzzle collector, you will find the metal, paper, and wood sections most helpful. Pay special attention to the care and handling of each material.

Exercise caution. At the first sign of trouble—or better yet, the moment you anticipate trouble—stop. Think about what you are doing. Then call a professional and place the job in the hands of an expert.

Insuring Your Collection

You have already taken the first steps to safeguarding your toys, games, and puzzles by keeping an adequate set of records and displaying and storing the items properly. These are your first lines of defense. Your collection is not insured without them.

You should make a photographic record of the collection as a whole. A Polaroid, 35mm, or video camera will be fine. Stand in the center of each room in which your collection is housed and take a series of pictures as you turn in a complete circle. Make two sets: one for yourself and one for your insurance agent. Again, make certain to store these records in a location separate from the toys, games, and puzzles that they document.

Before you spend any money for insurance, put a security plan into effect. Security must be addressed on two fronts. The first is you and your family. Do not talk about your collection of toys, games, and puzzles in public. You certainly should share your love for them, but do so discreetly. Whenever you have visitors, tell them that you would be appreciative if they did not discuss your collection with acquaintances. Tell this to collectors as well. They should know better, but they often find it hard to resist bragging that they have seen someone's collection.

The second front is an adequate home security system against theft and fire. There are a wide variety of systems available. You can employ a security consultant to help plan a system, but probably will be just as well served by talking with your local police and fire officials and your insurance agent, and then requesting competitive bids from local security firms. Investing in a security system also will save you money on your insurance premiums.

Once you have provided these safeguards for your toys, games, and puzzles, it is time to consider insurance against both damage (breakage) and loss. Do not forget to inquire about both.

In all probability your homeowner's policy provides some content protection. The amount is often a percentage of the value of the house. In most cases, it will be inadequate to cover the value of your collection. The solution is to purchase special insurance protection. Many individuals already have insurance riders for jewelry, furs, and weapons. Protection for your toys, games, and puzzles, along with the supporting paper ephemera, is obtained through fine arts and valuable paper insurance riders.

A fine arts rider covers fine arts and decorative accessories. A valuable paper rider applies to books and paper ephemera. When deciding on what amount of coverage is appropriate, do not forget the value of your research library and files. There are two levels of coverage: breakage and loss. Loss coverage is essential. Breakage is optional and depends greatly on the class of objects being insured.

Once again, valuable advice can be found in the literature prepared for museum professionals. Read Chapter 9, ''Insurance,'' in Dudley and Wilkinson's *Museum Registration Methods*. In fact, you can save time by asking the librarian to copy the chapter for you and mail it. Pay in advance by check if there are any costs.

Choosing the right insurance agent is your key to good coverage. There are specialists in this field, such as Huntington T. Block and John B. Lawton of Huntington T. Block Insurance, 2101 L Street NW, Washington, DC 20037–1585. However, your best bet usually is a local insurance agent. Since you are likely to be adding to and subtracting from your insurance policy on a regular basis, having someone nearby to talk to makes sense. Check with your local museum or historical society to see who they use; such an agent already is familiar with fine-arts and valuable paper coverage and the various options open to you.

Filing requirements differ from company to company, as do rates. A local agent is in a position to shop around for a set of reporting requirements and costs that fit your specific needs. The more you work with your local agent, the more educated and interested he becomes.

In almost every case, you will be asked to prepare an appraisal of your collection. Most insurance companies will not accept a list of values prepared by you, even though you are in the best position to know what your things are worth. Professional appraisers are not inexpensive. Their hourly rates can compare to those of attorneys or accountants. You can save time and money by preparing a list of your collection in advance so that the appraiser only has to check your descriptions and add the appropriate values. An alternative to an appraiser is a leading toy, game, and puzzle collector.

Whether you use a professional appraiser or fellow collector to assess the values, make certain that your report to the insurance company contains a list of the qualifications of the person doing the valuation. The company's biggest concern is whether it is insuring for a fair replacement value.

The balance of this section will focus on fine arts insurance, the form most used by toy, game, and puzzle collectors. In almost every case, the same information applies to valuable paper insurance.

Fine-arts insurance is treated as inland marine or inland transportation insurance so that the underwriters are not restricted to narrow lines of coverage. The best form of fine-arts insurance is an all-risk policy, which covers you against ''all risks of physical loss or damage from any external cause except as herein excluded.''

Since underwriters have flexibility in the type of coverage they write under a fine-arts policy, you can obtain a policy tailored to your specific needs. The following are some points you will want to consider:

1. The policy should cover your toys, games, and puzzles not only on the premises but also in transit, from the time you buy or acquire them to the time they reach the hands of their next owner(s).
2. The policy should be based on the value of each toy, game, or puzzle, not on the value of the whole collection. This forces you to have adequate records to justify the amount of insurance that you seek. It is possible to obtain coverage based on a stated or ''flat'' amount, but this option should be exercised only when the cost of insuring individual objects becomes prohibitive.
3. The policy should have provisions for adding and subtracting objects. A policy can be written so that your acquisition sheets are listed as the ''records of the insured.'' This approach can provide the flexibility you may need.
4. Explore the deductible options that are availa-

ble. A deductible clause often can reduce rates. If you are investing in expensive items, a $100 or $500 deductible clause reduces the number of small claims and paperwork.

5. Does the insurer offer a "pair" and "set" value provision? If your collection contains objects in sets or pairs where damage to one piece can seriously affect the value of the other(s), you must provide for this type of protection. With the pair-and-set coverage, the insurance company pays for all the objects in a set, provided they can take the undamaged ones that remain. Some negotiating is allowed.
6. Does the policy provide for "mysterious disappearance?" Most policies require that theft be proved. A policy with a mysterious-disappearance clause allows a little more flexibility.
7. Does the policy allow the option of repairing or replacing the object with a "substantially identical" object? You should avoid such a policy, since "substantially identical" may mean one thing to you and another to your insurer.
8. Is there a discount for a security and fire alarm system? If so, does the amount of the discount depend on the type of system installed? Are there any additional safeguards that will further reduce the premium?
9. Under what circumstances may the insurer cancel the policy? You need to make certain that your policy will not be canceled after your first loss.

The cost of a fine arts policy is based on a fixed fee per $100 of value, per month or per year. However, writing fine arts policies for toys, games, and puzzles is still in its infancy, and rates vary widely from company to company. Insist that your agent contact several companies.

Experience has shown that the losses on fine arts insurance are small. Companies that write a lot of fine arts policies usually offer the best rates because they have developed actuarial tables that identify their risk. Most importantly, insure with a company with an established reputation.

When you are about to purchase a policy, you should insist that your agent review every clause with you. You may also want to ask your attorney and accountant to review the policy. You also want to stress confidentiality. Do not hesitate to ask your agent how his records are stored. Request that your policy receive limited exposure among his office staff.

Make certain to obtain two copies of your policy, and keep them in separate locations. If your insurer loses your policy and you lose your copy too, you still have the other.

Finally, be careful not to become insurance-poor. The amount spent on insurance must be justified. Perhaps your wisest plan is to insure only the premier objects in your collection and take your chances on the ordinary objects. The latter are easier to replace.

The simple precautions listed above will not limit the joy that you find surrounding yourself with toys, games, and puzzles. In all likelihood, they will probably enhance it through the peace of mind created by knowing you have acted responsibly.

CHAPTER 7

Researching Toys, Games, and Puzzles

Part of the fun of collecting toys, games, and puzzles is learning more about them. Every toy has a wealth of stories to tell: Who designed it? Who made it? How was it made? How was it packaged? How was it advertised? How was it sold? Who bought it? How was it used? How does it relate to similar objects made by the same manufacturer and by other manufacturers? Why was it saved? What does it say about the person who collected it? Once you develop this type of inquiring mind about your toys, games, and puzzles, you transform them from inanimate to animate objects. No wonder collectors fall in love with their toys.

Finding answers to these questions is not as easy as it might sound. You have to become a toy, game, and puzzle detective. Your investigation will take you off the beaten track. You will meet some very unusual, but not necessarily unsavory, characters. Your principal reward will be the fact that you are the first collector to crack the case.

Start by trying to learn about the manufacturer. The initial information is often located on the toy, game, or puzzle or on its box. Watch out. Sometimes the information relates to the distributor, not the manufacturer. The box for *In Blossom Time*, Miss America Puzzle Series No. 4, states: "Distributed exclusively by The American News Company, Inc., and Branches." Well and good, but who made it? Be highly suspicious of manufacturers listed at 200, 500, or 520 Fifth Avenue, New York City. Although these buildings do or did house corporate offices of some manufacturers, they also serve as the addresses for many manufacturers' representatives. If the box contains licensing information, make a note of it. It will come in handy later.

Once you have identified the manufacturer, start by checking the manufacturer listings in Richard O'Brien's *Collecting Toys: A Collector's Identification and Value Guide, No. 5*, Robert Friz's *The Official Price Guide to Collectible Toys, Fourth Edition*, Lee Dennis' *Warman's Antique American Games, 1840–1940*, and Anne Williams' *Jigsaw Puzzles: An Illustrated History and Price Guide*. Books have been published about a number of toy manufacturers, including Dinky, Lehmann, Matchbox, and Marx. You are seeking the basics: (1) correct name of the manufacturer; (2) location of corporate offices and factories; (3) working dates; and (4) some idea of the toys, games, or puzzles the manufacturer made.

Fig. 7-1 One of the first questions any collector asks about a toy is who made it. In this case, the answer is Marx.

Fig. 7-2 A reference librarian in Pittsburgh, Pennsylvania, is the ideal person to provide some preliminary information about the Spear Department Store.

Libraries and Historical Societies

You do not need to go into the field to take the next step. Pick up your telephone. First, call the reference librarian at your local library or the librarian at your local historical society and ask them to provide you with the name and addresses of historical societies, museums, and newspapers for the area in which the manufacturer is located. Second, call telephone information and get the phone number for the nearest public library. Contact the library first, the historical societies and museums second. Hold the newspaper information until later.

When calling the library, ask for the reference librarian. Explain that you are trying to obtain information about a toy, game, or puzzle manufacturer for research purposes. Remember, the more information that you can provide the reference librarian, the better she is going to be able to help you. If you already have rough working dates, you might suggest that city directories be consulted. Do not expect the librarian to find the information immediately. Indicate that you would be willing to call back a day or two later, after she has had a chance to do research.

In most cases, the reference librarian will unearth useful information. Rather than have the information communicated to you over the telephone, ask if it can be photocopied and sent. Always offer to pay. This ensures that you get all the information and get it accurately.

Do not abuse the reference librarian; she is not your personal servant. You should expect her to devote minutes to your question, not hours. If hours are required, you must go to the library and do the research yourself.

When speaking to the reference librarian, ask for her assessment of the library's holdings as a potential information source if more detailed research is necessary. Also inquire about three additional areas: (1) the holdings and appropriate personnel to contact at the local historical societies

Fig. 7-3 This advertising puzzle provides dates which would be useful to a reference librarian.

and museums, (2) names of other individuals who have asked about the company, and (3) names and addresses of any former employees of the company she may know of. Do not forget to get the name of the reference librarian and address of the library. Thank you notes are very appropriate, along with a donation to the library if the service and results are extraordinary.

Collectors, Dealers and Factories

About the same time you approach the library, start contacting collectors and dealers in the field who have large research holdings or an interest in other products made by the same manufacturer. Check the collector-dealer file that you maintain. In order to secure their assistance, you must be prepared to share your findings. Swapping research information in the toy, game, and puzzle field is very much a two-way endeavor.

Next, approach the local newspapers. The first step is a letter to the editor. Explain your research efforts and ask anyone with information to contact you. The chances that your letter will be published are about one in four. If you have not received any response within two weeks, place an advertisement in the classified section making the same request. The final step is to contact the newspaper city desk editor to ask if a reporter could be assigned to write a story about your research. This approach works best when you can supply the reporter with a fairly large amount of information about the manufacturer.

This preliminary research work takes approximately a month. Once you have received the data from all these sources, you will be in an excellent position to decide if a trip to where the toy, game, or puzzle was made is worthwhile. In almost every case, the answer is "yes."

When doing field research at a manufacturer's home town, never plan to spend only hours. It takes a minimum of one to two full days. Once again, your first stop is the library. A number of key sources that you want to check are county and city histories and anniversary publications, chamber of commerce publications, city and county directories, atlases (especially Sanborn insurance atlases), and subject and newspaper clipping files.

The real treasures are manufacturer's catalogs. Finding them in a library or a historical society's files sometimes calls for creative thinking. Historical societies usually file catalogs by manufacturer. Do not fail to check the card catalog; sometimes they are cataloged as books and shelved with the general collection. Libraries tend to file them by subject matter. The key is, what subject? They might be under iron manufacturers if the toys were made of cast iron. "Child's playthings" is an oft-found category. When trying to track down information on TUCO (The Upson Company) puzzles,

I found the information at one library under "building materials." The Upson Company's primary product was wallboard.

Photocopy everything of interest. Forget the expense, even if it is 25 cents or more a sheet. You want accuracy. Just think about many times you misspelled something when taking hand written notes.

Do not focus on the manufacturer alone. Among the first information that you will uncover are the names of owners, managers, and designers. Begin checking for information about them in published genealogies and in genealogical files. Factories did not design and make toys, games, and puzzles; people did. Factories only housed the equipment—the people are the real story.

Prior to your trip, place a note in the local paper to inform the members of the community that you are coming, what you will be doing, and where you will be staying. Take a portable tape recorder as part of your traveling gear. If you are lucky, you will already have a file of several names from earlier efforts.

Wait to talk with former factory owners, managers, designers, and assembly line workers until after you have done your research at the libraries. You uncover basic information at libraries, not through personal interviews. You want the interviews to provide personal nuances, information that breathes life into the story. Further, you will elicit far more information from the interview if you can impress the person you are interviewing with your knowledge of the manufacturer's background.

The most common mistake made by the inexperienced interviewer is leading the interviewee. Do not ask questions that suggest the answer you are seeking; do not dominate the interview by telling what you have found and expressing your opinion on what it means; and do not continually correct faulty memory. Let the person talk. It is the interviewee's memories that you are seeking.

So far, we have assumed that the manufacturer is no longer in business. This is not always true. The company may have survived, possibly changing hands several times in the interim. Finding that a manufacturer survives is great news, but it doesn't guarantee you any breakthroughs.

Manufacturers are concerned primarily about the present and future—sales, profit, and future product. It is the exceptional manufacturer that cares about its past. Ten or 20 years ago is ancient history in modern American manufacturing. Few companies are concerned enough about their past to maintain an ongoing file of their sales catalogs, let alone a company archive. The best you can hope for is a sympathetic ear somewhere in the corporate structure.

When contacting a company, always ask for the public relations department first. Chances are that your request will not be the first one they have received. In smaller companies that have no public relations personnel, you usually talk to the sales manager, who tends to view you as a pain in the neck because you do not want to buy something. Getting a positive response here is a test of your human relations skills.

Keep your pitch short. Briefly describe the whats and whys of your research. Ask four basic questions:

1. Does the company have an archive and is it open to outside researchers?

2. If there is no archive, does the company maintain a file of its old sales catalogs and products?

3. Are there any employees still with the company who were employed there when the toy, game, or puzzle that you are researching was manufactured?

4. If the company is still making similar products, would it be possible to tour the plant?

Please understand the reluctance of companies to deal with the toy, game, or puzzle researcher. You are not paying them. Someone must be reassigned from other duties to assist you, which can be a problem if the company is a small one. Competition in the toy, game, and puzzle market is fierce. Great reluctance should be expected when requesting information on production figures and future products.

Information is fine, but the thing that brought you to the manufacturer's town is a specific toy, game, or puzzle—just the type of thing factory workers took home for their children. Hunt some goodies at the same time that you are hunting information. Again, the best method is an advertisement in the local paper. The more specific the advertisement, the more precise the results. Do not be modest; mention that you are there to buy.

One shrewd collector always contacts the local library and/or historical society in advance and offers to present a program on the manufacturer. Attendees are invited to bring toys, games, and puzzles for a free appraisal. Of course, the appraisal offer is a thinly disguised buying ploy. But you must understand that in this situation you will be competing with the historical society and area collectors who want to prevent their local products from gravitating to an outside home.

To whomever you speak, ask one more basic question: "Do you know anyone around these parts who collects—?" In a short time, you should have leads to several local collectors. Contact them and ask if you can meet with them. As a collector yourself, you understand how reluctant you are to provide months or years of research to someone who shows up on your doorstep and simply says, "Give me everything you've got." If you lack information to exchange, count on your enthusiasm and charm to get you through. If you have uncovered new information, share it with the person sharing with you. Make it clear if you plan to publish the results of your research. Give credit where credit is due. Do not hesitate to tell the person to whom you are giving newly discovered choice research data that this is for their eyes alone.

Once you have found out all you can about the manufacturer, it is time to tackle some of the other questions the toy, game, or puzzle poses. Finding a patent number or date is exceptionally good fortune. Call your local library to find the library nearest you that serves as a U.S. Government depository. It has copies of the patent records either in printed form or on microfilm. If it is close, go and do the research.

Fig. 7-4 Many mechanical banks have a patent number.

If the depository is some distance, you can obtain a photocopy of the patent by writing the U.S. Patent and Trademark Office, Washington, DC 20231. The more information you send, the more you increase your chances of getting the patent or trademark information that you seek. Ideally, you should send the patent number, date of patent (if known), name of patentee, and a brief description of the toy, game, or puzzle. Photocopy information that will help in the search. Send a photograph if you think it important. There are basically two types of patents, utility patents and design patents. In 1991 the fee is $1.50 for each patent ordered. The U.S. Patent and Trademark Office publishes *Obtaining Information from Patents, Patent Clas-*

sification and Search Services. Write for a copy for your files.

It is helpful to understand how thc toys, games, or puzzles that you collect were manufactured. If the manufacturer that made them is no longer in business, contact manufacturers of similar toys, games, or puzzles and ask if a plant tour can be arranged. Make certain to see the packaging and distribution system as well as the actual manufacturing process. Seeing the assembly line process at work gives you a far better appreciation for the number of toys produced.

Trade Associations

Leading trade organizations are also excellent sources of information.

The Toy Manufacturers of America (200 Fifth Ave., New York, NY 10010) is the leading toy, game, and puzzle manufacturers trade organization. In the trade, 200 Fifth Ave. is known as the "Toy Building." In addition to serving as headquarters for the association, it houses the national corporate offices for some manufacturers and provides space for representatives from other companies. The Toy Manufacturers Association sponsors the annual New York Toy Fair, open only to members of the trade and the press.

Playthings (51 Madison Ave., New York, NY 10010) serves as the unofficial trade journal for the toy industry. The monthly magazine was founded in January 1903 and is still being published. In addition to 12 information-packed issues, the annual subscription of $22 (1991 price) brings you *Playthings Directory*, which lists manufacturers, manufacturers' representatives, inventors, and designers.

Playthings is a gold mine of information. Back issues chronicle the history of the toy industry in the 20th century. If you know the exact date your toy was first manufactured, check the issues of *Playthings* six months before and six months after for information. If you have only an approximate date, you will have to cover a broader time span. A similar publication *Toys and Novelties* (later *Toys and Bicycles*), began in 1909 and lasted for several decades. Make a point to locate the library nearest you that has a full run of these two periodicals.

Toy and Hobby World (463 7th Ave., New York, NY 10018) is an excellent research source for more recent toys. In addition to printing information about newly released toys, the magazine also features articles on toy safety and the state of the toy market.

Sources of Specific Information

Finding answers for the questions about how a toy was packaged, advertised, sold, and who bought it involves basically the same sources. You should have an excellent idea of the original packaging, since you bought your toy, game, or puzzle along with its original box. If not, do not fret. Many advertisements show the packaging as well as the product.

One line of inquiry might might be the national children's and adult magazines of the era. Of course, these are helpful only if the toy, game, or puzzle had a national potential market. If not, try the hometown and regional newspapers. There are dealers who specialize in supplying collectors with magazine and newspaper advertising relating to their favorite collectible. They advertise in *PCM* and exhibit at paper shows.

Other sources are the catalogs of large department stores and mail order merchandisers. Alas, toys, games, and puzzles receive short shrift in the general catalogs. Companies such as Sears, Roebuck & Co. and Marshall Field issued separate toy catalogs in the fall. Likewise, department stores large and small distributed Christmas "wish books," many of which were stock pieces provided by toy distributors. They should always be checked.

Company broadsides (flyers), brochures, catalogs, and merchandising kits also are an important source. These are the items that were sent to distributors and toy buyers. Miniature versions were often packaged in the company's other products, especially in the months before and immediately after Christmas. A surprising number survive, due in part to the archives of department stores, where old catalogs tend to get boxed and put into storage rather than thrown out. Many collectors have made arrangements with store toy buyers in their areas to obtain all obsolete toy catalogs that the buyers want to discard.

Point-of-purchase broadsides, signs, and display units are wonderful items to support a toy, game, or puzzle collection. It was common practice for department stores to run pictures of their toy departments as part of their Christmas advertising. The larger stores often photo-documented their ''Toylands.'' A surprising number of these photographs survive. These are excellent research sources for determining what material was used for advertising purposes.

Be prepared to compete financially for advertising material. In the 1970s collecting all forms of advertising objects (e.g., pocket mirrors, trays, signs, etc.) became almost a national pastime. Advertising collectors generally collect by type of object or by manufacturer. Their principal value considerations are pizzazz of image, scarcity, and age. Toy advertising in particular has strong appeal to the advertising collector because of its imagery.

There is no collectors' club devoted exclusively to advertising. The closest organization is the Tin Container Collectors Association (P.O. Box 440101, Aurora, CA 80014), a strong dealer-based organization, many of whose members handle a much broader range of advertising products than tin containers. Just as there are specialized toy shows, so also are there specialized advertising shows, sometimes combined with paper shows. You should attend one or two shows each year to widen your dealer contacts. While advertising collectors and dealers do advertise in *PCM*, you might also consider subscribing to *PAC* (P.O. Box 500, Mt. Joy, PA 17552), a newspaper that claims to be the journal of the National Association of Paper and Advertising Collectibles (NAPAC). The ''association'' has no officers or meetings, nothing but the paper itself.

In order to determine how a toy, game, or puzzle was used, you must play with it. It sounds easy, and usually it is. However, if a toy is missing parts, a game its instructions, or a mystery puzzle its story booklet, you have trouble. Fortunately, most of these troubles can be resolved through the aid of another collector or one of the collectors' clubs.

Playing with a toy as an adult is not quite the same as playing with a toy as a child. Each brings a very different set of values to the activity. If you really want to see how a toy was played with, turn it over to a child. (If the toy costs in the hundreds of dollars, however, few collectors are willing to take the risk.)

A resource much overlooked by toy, game, and puzzle researchers is photographs. Children play with toys, games, and puzzles and opening their packages under the Christmas tree have been favorite family photo opportunities for nearly a century. Whenever you see a pile of stereoscopic views, go through them. Not all were commercially produced—there were plenty of privately made views. Develop a strong relationship with postcard dealers. Between 1910 and 1940, it was quite common to print multiple copies of photographs on postcard stock. These were sent to friends or passed around for family albums. Two excellent places to advertise for non-commercial postcards picturing children playing with toys, games, and puzzles are *Barr's Postcard News* (700 South Sixth St., Lansing, IA 52151) and *Postcard Collector* (Joe Jones Publishing, P.O. Box 337, Iola, WI 54945). When attending an auction or flea market, look through the piles of black-and-white family photographs from the 1930s through the present. Buy any pictures showing children playing with readily identifiable toys, games, or puzzles, whether you collect them or not. The ones of no interest to you make excellent gifts or trading material for other collectors.

The relationship between like objects is easy to see in a theme collection, such as TV board games or cap pistols. It is less likely to be apparent if the collection is more singly focused, such as toys, games, and puzzles made by Marx or Hopalong Cassidy items. Few toys, games, or puzzles exist in a vacuum. Success draws imitators. Collectors gain insight by knowing how their toys relate to similar toys from other manufacturers.

The most immediate area of comparison is quality. Some toys, games, and puzzles were simply made better than others. At which level do the items in your collection belong? Perhaps they are not quite as great as you thought they were. Collectors always look at their toys through rose-colored glasses. A little reevaluation every now and then never hurts.

Identifying the competition allows you to understand better the marketing strategy used to sell your toys, games, or puzzles. The rise of the American Thermos Company as a leading manufacturer of character lunch kits, had a great deal to do with a restrictive clause in Aladdin's contract with William Boyd, which read: "You further agree that you will not manufacture, sell or distribute any [article] . . . which is identified with or bears the name of any living or dead person of prominence or any cowboy personality." American Thermos Company obtained the Roy Rogers license, and the rest, as they say, is history.

Companies do not promote all products equally. Your research with company catalogs and sales literature will provide clues as to how the company itself viewed the toy, game, or puzzle that you are researching. Remember, you are hardly objective. Try as you might to exclude it, love for your toys very much influences how you see and interpret information. Accept the truth, no matter how hard it is.

There are no definitive answers as to why some toys, games, and puzzles are saved and others are discarded. Ask a hundred different individuals, and get a hundred different answers. By the time you acquire most of the toys in your collection, they have passed through several hands. The information about why they were saved is lost.

Thus, when acquiring an item from its original owner, the serious collector has a special responsibility to ask why that toy, game, or puzzle was saved. Record the answer carefully. Also, query the owner for any favorite stories about the toy. If the original owner is talkative, ask: when was the toy acquired, how often was it played with, who aside from the owner played with it, how was it stored, when was the last time it was played with, and what led to its rediscovery. Why is this so important? Just as it is helpful for you to understand the thought processes that govern you and other collectors, it is equally critical to understand original toy owners. If your goal is to convince them to sell you their toys, the better you understand them, the greater your chances of success.

The toys, games, and puzzles that we collect reflect our own personalities. There is no way to avoid it. If you tell someone you collect puzzles, an image is brought to mind. If you clarify your remark to say you collect only puzzles with a military theme, a far different image is conjured. It is unlikely that anyone is ever going to obtain a government grant to study collectors, but it might prove to be an interesting exercise.

It is dangerous to think in stereotypes. Collectors of toys, games, and puzzles come from a broad spectrum of humanity. But stereotypes do exist, and may even have some basis in truth. Be alert to them, and do not allow them to control your thoughts.

Not every toy, game, or puzzle collector does research. The number is actually less than half. Pity the majority; they do not know the fun they are missing. Don't become one of them.

Once you have completed your research, share it. Summarize your findings and send a copy to every individual and institution that helped you. Lecture at collectors' clubs, shows, and on the local rubber-chicken circuit. Write an article or series of articles for one of the trade periodicals. If the information warrants, consider writing a book. It is becoming more and more difficult to find a publisher for monographs about toys, games, and puzzles, but they do exist. Be persistent.

Finally, take time out to pat yourself on the back and celebrate. You have saved a bit of the past.

CHAPTER 8

The International Market

When you visit Europe, browse the antiques and collectibles section in the bookshops. You will notice two things. The first is a rather large number of books published in America. The second is a strong interest in the subject of toys.

Europeans want to know what Americans collect and what they pay. Until the mid-1980s, they used this knowledge defensively. American dealers were scouting European flea markets, antiques shops, and shows for collectibles—a large number of which were toys—for resale to American collectors. The Europeans wanted a fair return. Knowing values on the American toy, game, and puzzle market helped them set prices.

In the mid-1980s this posture changed. Europeans became the aggressors. Books about American collectibles turned into shopping catalogs. They drooled over them much like a farm wife drools over the Sears, Roebuck catalog. The flow of toys was reversed. Instead of Americans raiding the European markets, Europeans began raiding the American market.

Europeans had been collecting toys for decades, but with a nationalistic orientation. Germans collected German-manufactured toys, the French sought toys by French manufacturers, etc. Only the British had broadened their interests to include puzzles. Collectors focused primarily on late 19th century and early 20th century toys. Toys made after World War I were looked down upon as "too recent."

Until the mid-1970s, European toy collecting was centered in the upper class, fueled in part by a strong belief in toys as great investments against inflation. This emphasis is still extremely strong in the European collecting community. Rumors are rampant that a European collector-investor paid more than $1,000,000 for a Charles hose reel made by George Brown in Forrestville, Conn., in the 1870s.

In the late 1980s Mint & Boxed (110 High Street, Edgware, Middlesex HA8 7HF England) began issuing full color catalogs of high-priced investment-grade toys. Their advertisements state, "Every toy, whether tinplate or die-cast is top quality and an assured future asset." Prices start in the thousands. The company was expected to open a New York showroom on Madison Avenue, having lured Eric Alberta away from Christie's East to direct it.

The big news, however, is not the growth at the top end of the European toy market, but the enormous expansion of collectors in the middle-market and low-end sectors. There are several contributing factors.

In addition, European collectors have discovered 20th century collectibles and have fallen in love with their affordability. Gone are the prejudices against things less than several hundred years old. Today's European collectors are motivated by exactly the same forces that drive their American cousins.

Toys trade briskly at European flea markets and auctions. The London International Antique Toy and Doll Convention and Parmobile's Paris Toymania held each year in May attract collectors from Europe, America, and elsewhere around the world. Each month *Antique Toy World*'s calendar listings include "Show and Auction Dates—European Countries and Great Britain." A quick perusal shows a toy meet somewhere on the continent almost every weekend. *Toy Shop* also includes a section for "Canada and Foreign" (95 percent of which is European) in its "Show Directory."

Fig. 8-1 Margaret Davies exhibited a large collection of children's books at a recent London toy show.

If only the Europeans would stay home! Fat chance. European collectors and dealers recognize that America is the great motherlode for toys, games, and puzzles. More and more hunting expeditions are being organized as America is increasingly viewed as ripe for the plucking.

Think back to my earlier statement that after World War II, the entire world was influenced by American movies, American television, and American music. A great many toys, games, and puzzles can be identified with at least one of these three cross-cultural phenomena. The Germans loved Bonanza. Little wonder why Ben and the boys are part of many Germans' toy collections. The worldwide export of toys is larger than most collectors realize. Licensing also reaches across international borders. European toys after the 1960s very much resemble their American counterparts.

It is impossible to pick up a toy periodical without noticing several advertisements from European dealers. Mr. Mercedes (Kent, England), John and Simon Haley Collectors Old Toyshop (Halifax, England), Mint & Boxed (Edgware, England), Galerie Andre (Brussels, Belgium), Wolfgang Morian (Inning, Germany), Historic Toy Marketing (Dusseldorf, Germany), George Shulz (Duisburg, Germany), Bagatelle (Thonon, France), and Tut Tut (Amsterdam, Netherlands) had box advertisements in the August 1990 edition of *Antique Toy World*. They were joined by three Canadian dealers (Giesela Antiques, Toronto; Syldon Antique Toys, Edwards; and Mike's General Store, Manitoba), one Australian dealer (J. Cervenka, Bullaburra), and one Japanese dealer (Yuji Sakamoto, Tokyo). This indication of international interest in the American toy, game, and puzzle market is just the tip of the iceberg.

Foreign dealers are feeling their way. Many of

their advertisements solicit American buyers. The more aggressive list their wants and ask for American contacts. The number of foreign dealers attending American toy shows has more than tripled in the last year alone. The early 1990s are expected to be a time of "first" contacts. It is commonly believed that European raiders will overrun the American market by the mid-1990s.

Prices for toys, games, and puzzles now differ very little between America and Europe. While this bodes ill for the dealer, it allows the collector to travel abroad and make some excellent purchases. Northstar Tours (P.O. Box 810, Lakeville, MN 55044) runs a "European Toytour" each spring. Most collectors prefer to travel on their own. Peter B. Manston's *Manston's Flea Markets, Antique Fairs and Auctions of Britain*, *Manston's Flea Markets, Antique Fairs and Auctions of France*, and *Manston's Flea Markets, Antique Fairs and Auctions of Germany*, all available from Travel Keys (P.O. Box 160691, Sacramento, CA 95816), are invaluable. If you are headed for England, also obtain a copy of Robert and Harriett Swedberg's *Antiquing in England* (Wallace-Homestead, 1989).

Fig. 8-2 Outdoor markets on a weekly basis are part of the European antiquing scene.

Do not misinterpret this heavy emphasis on Europe. The toy, game, and puzzle market is truly international. Toy collectors are found worldwide. Mediterranean and South American collectors are making their presence felt at auctions and shows. However, it is the Japanese that are blazing the 21st century toy collecting trail.

The Japanese have attracted worldwide attention because of their successful activities in the fine arts market. They are also the major players in the battery-operated, friction, and windup toy markets. Initially, their collecting emphasis was on acquiring Japanese-manufactured toys from the 1920s and 1930s, and the Japanese exports from the post-war period. Japanese pickers and dealers came to America prepared to pay whatever it took to acquire them. No price was too high; collectors back in Japan were willing to pay more. A wave of Japanese buying occurred in the early 1980s, tapered off in the mid-1980s, but resumed at an even higher level and more accelerated pace in 1990.

The Japanese public is learning about toys, games, and puzzles through lavishly illustrated, full-color coffee table books featuring the collections of major Japanese collectors. Attracted by what they see, many readers become collectors. Few of these books reach the American market. One of the rare exceptions is Teruhisa Kitahara's three-volume set, *Yesterday's Toys* (Chronicle Books, 1988). The first volume covers celluloid dolls, clowns, and animals; the second looks at planes, trains, boats, and cars; and the third features robots, spaceships, astronauts, and monsters. Kitahara, born in 1948, has a collection of more than 10,000 tin toys from the period 1900 to 1960 and serves as curator of the Tin Toy Museum in Yokohama and Harajuku, Japan.

Collecting toys of their own manufacture only whetted the appetite of Japanese collectors. Once involved in the toy, game, and puzzle market, it did not take them long to discover the wonderful opportunities marketwide. Japanese toy collectors are now every bit as sophisticated and have interests just as broad as their American and European counterparts. They represent an important subscriber base for all American toy periodicals.

It is a little late to emulate Paul Revere and ride through the toy auctions and shows shouting, "The British are coming, the British are coming!" The truth is, the British—and other toy collectors from around the world—are here. Accept the fact that toys, games, and puzzles are part of an international market. Make contact with collectors and dealers outside the United States. Offer to pick for them—they need someone on the scene.

However, free trade should be fair trade. Get copies of their toy, game, and puzzle price guides and other literature to determine what they are paying at home, then set your prices accordingly. A good time can be had by all.

CHAPTER 9

State of the Market

While the toy, game, and puzzle market is no longer in its infancy, it has not yet reached maturity. Do not be deceived by appearances. Although there are many traditional elements, they are in the minority. The bulk of the players are young. If anything, the toy, game, and puzzle market is in its adolescent stage—vibrant, excitable, opportunistic, aggressive, and brash.

One can draw an analogy between it and the United States in the 1880s. There was an older portion with strong beliefs and tradition (tin and cast iron toy collectors), a middle that was beginning to stabilize and play a major role (lithographed tin and game collectors), and a frontier where all hell was breaking loose (action figures and pedal car collectors). Traditionalists appear content to let the youngsters run. As the toy, game, and puzzle market emerged from the 1980s, it was racing.

The previous chapter explored the growing international aspects of the toy, game, and puzzle market. However, as the 1990s begin, the overwhelming majority of American toy, game, and puzzle collectors continue to focus on the national market. The fact that there is a national market at all says a great deal about the changes in the toy, game, and puzzle market in the 1980s. A national market exists because there is pricing consistency across the country, nationwide interaction among dealers and collectors through auctions, shows, collectors' clubs, and personal contacts, and an established and expanding body of literature, including books, periodicals and, most importantly, price guides. The 1980s witnessed these elements being put into place; the 1990s will see them grow and mature.

Toys

The toy market split apart in the 1980s. Specialization became the only way to build a meaningful collection in a world of rapidly escalating prices for almost everything. The great toy collections assembled by giants such as Perelman and Barenholtz covered a broad range of toys. As the 1980s came to a close these collections were dispersed, marking the beginning of the end of the era of the mid-20th century "classic" toy collector.

In upscale toys, the leadership of the collector is being challenged by the investor, and the investor appears to be winning. The problem with investors is attitude. To them the toy no longer is an object of affection, but rather a commodity to be bought and sold, much like a side of beef. Prices are highly speculative and trendy. Toys are not

Fig. 9-1 This set was sold at Phillips in New York for $2,200. At this price, these toy soldiers are entering the investment stage.

fine art, yet the prevailing attitudes that govern the fine arts market have worked their way into upscale toys. It is time for a closer look at what is happening.

The degree of specialization in the toy market is astonishing. Vehicle collectors now subdivide into automobiles, buses, motorcycles, fire equipment, trucks, and horse-drawn vehicles, with large collections built around just one of these subthemes. Further, there is a growing tendency to specialize by date, dividing roughly into three periods: pre-1920, 1920–45, and post-1945. Each has its loyalists and appropriate degree of snobbery.

More new categories reached "respectability" among collectors in the 1980s than in any previous decade. Among the newcomers were action figures, battery-operated toys, cap pistols (an old timer that finally fired), Fisher-Price toys, Japanese tin, Matchbox toys, plastic model kits (especially Aurora figure kits), television-related toys, and World War II toys. Previously, it took 25 to 30 years from the time of manufacture to the time of collectibility. That period was reduced to 15 to 20 years in the 1980s. Early indications are that it will be reduced even further in the 1990s. Dealers were already advertising Roger Rabbit material in the August 1990 issue of *Toy Shop*.

In 1990 the toy market was deriving more than

Fig. 9-2 Matchbox toys became an established collecting category in the late 1980s.

two-thirds of its energy from toys made after World War II—check any issue of *Toy Shop*. The balance is still about fifty-fifty between pre- and post-war toys at toy shows. However, it is rapidly shifting in favor of the post-war material.

It would take several pages to list the "hot" post-1945 toy categories. Think of any toy from that period, and it probably would be on such a list. If your imagination is a bit rusty, here are a few not-so-obvious categories: bobbin head dolls, coloring books, Hanna-Barbera characters of all sorts, Peanuts collectibles, and Pez dispensers. In the 1990s the toy collector market is extremely broad—broader than most people realize. All indications are that it will become even broader.

A great many of the "hot" categories are highly speculative in nature. Perhaps this is why "old timer" toy collectors look disparagingly upon them. Think carefully before catching collecting fever for cereal boxes (no, they are not toys, but they are bought and sold actively in the toy market), GI Joe dolls and accessories, Masters of the Universe material, monsters, and Star Wars items. The market is currently working on the assumption that every toy is going to be collectible. Collectors and dealers alike are not allowing enough time for natural selection to weed out the undesirable toys.

The first major signs of trouble in Toytown began in late spring 1990. Dealers started complaining about the high cost of buying merchandise, a lack of customers, and an inability to meet expenses. The problem deepened by late summer, and in response, a slow but steady reduction in prices was begun, most noticeably in the post-1945 material. Buying at shows has been sporadic. The dealers that are doing well are selling directly to preferred customers via telephone and mail.

If the market recovers from the 1990 blues, the future should continue to be bright. If it does not, a three- to four-year recession may result. Many collectors and dealers are battening down the hatches; they see stormy times ahead.

Games

Games were the discovery of the 1980s. They went through a market run that saw prices rise rapidly and stabilize as the decade ended. Just like the toy market, the game market split into a series of niche markets, each with a life of its own.

The big winners in the 1980s price run were games made between 1890 and 1915 that had bright, pizzazzy, aesthetically appealing lithographed covers. Their prices begin in the hundreds and range into the thousands of dollars. A number of high-ticket games became sensations, the most famous being McLoughlin's "The Game Of Man In The Moon." These games became *objets d'art* in the eyes of many collectors and dealers. The current prognosis is that these games have reached their top value and are going to remain stable in the years ahead.

The 1980s price run identified a number of game categories where collectors in other areas were more responsible for determining market price than the game collectors. The most obvious is baseball theme games; however, all sports theme games do well. Transportation theme games and Disney games are two more categories with consistently active markets. Prices for these games should continue to show modest increases.

The real sleepers are games made between 1920 and 1940. Since there is little collector interest, prices remain low. The exceptions are games that

Fig. 9-3 Baseball games were one of the big winners in the 1980s game market.

feature a cartoon character, movie theme, or personality, and those licensed by Disney. Game collectors have begun to recognize the potential in the area. Prices should increase, but a full-blown run is not expected.

Game collectors are definitely divided into two camps: the pre-1940 collectors and the post-1940 collectors. Few collectors span the gap. The most vital growth in the game sector is occurring in the post-1940 area. An increasing number of game collectors are focusing on the period from 1945 to 1970. In addition, toy collectors who are attracted to the themes of these games buy them to supplement their collections. This competition is driving up prices. The average price for a 1950s boxed board game jumped from the $10 to $15 range in the mid-1980s to the $25 to $40 range in 1990.

Signs suggest an upcoming split within the post-1945 game collecting community. Vintage game collectors will focus on the 1950s and early 1960s. A second, much younger group will become active speculators in the wildly fluctuating collecting crazes that characterize 1970s and 1980s toys. Vintage games are likely to undergo another major price increase before stabilizing. Later games will continue their roller coaster ride through the 1990s.

The use of game boards for decorative purposes is still in its infancy. If this decorator trend gains popularity, the post-1920 game market will be strongly affected. The board itself will constitute 75 percent or more of the value of the game. Game collectors must be prepared to weather the craze if it comes. The good news is that it is not likely to last more than two to four years.

Reproductions and fakes are not yet a major problem in the game and puzzle sectors. However, the improving quality of the color photocopier means trouble ahead. In the 1990s, game collectors will have to pay far more attention to what they are buying than they did in the 1980s. They simply can no longer be certain the game is "period" just because it looks old. That look can be duplicated on a copier.

The 1980s witnessed the first price guide to games and the organization of a collectors' club. Additional general and specific game reference books and price guides will be published in the early 1990s. A quarterly publication on games was scheduled to begin late in 1990. The game collecting community was still unified in 1990, but this is likely to change by the end of the decade.

Puzzles

Puzzles promise to be the great discovery of the 1990s. One can make this prediction on affordability alone. The vast majority of puzzles still sell

Fig. 9-4 Some games are still selling at garage sale prices.

for less than $25. Dealers and collectors have shied away from puzzles for two reasons. First, they had no guide to collecting and valuing puzzles. Anne Williams' *Jigsaw Puzzles: An Illustrated History and Price Guide* should remedy that concern. Second, it is impossible to tell if a puzzle is complete without putting it together. This will always be a problem. However, as the value of puzzles increases, so does the incentive to put them together to check for completeness.

Puzzle collectors are still divided over what is the most important factor in pricing once completeness is established. Collectors tend to divide into wooden puzzle devotees and die-cut cardboard fanatics. One faction of the wood puzzle collectors values cutting skill over degree of difficulty, subject matter, or age. Other factions reorder these priorities. Die-cut cardboard puzzle collectors tend to agree that subject matter is the key element, but there are proponents of difficulty, age, and type.

At the moment all wooden puzzles are lumped together. Price is often assigned by the piece count. Average value per piece for a puzzle up to 250 pieces is five to 10 cents; for 250 pieces to 500 pieces, 10 to 15 cents; and for 500 pieces and more, 10 to 20 cents. Price variation is greatest among puzzles with larger numbers of pieces. Until the market becomes more sophisticated, this pricing approach works as well as any.

Wood puzzles were cut by many different makers, from large-scale commercial manufacturers such as Milton Bradley and Parker Brothers to the amateur woodworker using a jigsaw in his basement workshop at home. What unifies them is that each is unique. Few cutters traced a full cutting pattern. Cutters never repeated themselves. Dealers are beginning to charge a premium for puzzles they feel show quality cutting. However, the assumption that figural pieces mean quality is false. The puzzle as a whole must be studied to assess quality cutting. Opinions differ widely.

The greatest confusion rests with the scenic die-cut cardboard puzzle. Dealers are using age as a pricing criterion. The correct assumption to make is that most scenic die-cut cardboard puzzles made prior to 1940 are worth only a few dollars at best. Scenics made after that date are worth between 50 cents and $2. Puzzle collectors avoid scenics like the plague; so should you.

Today's most sought-after die-cut cardboard puzzles are advertising puzzles, Depression-era weekly puzzles, and special theme puzzles, such as mystery puzzles and World War II puzzles. Advertising puzzles show the greatest price range, from a few dollars to more than $100. Weekly puzzles average between $4 and $10. Special theme puzzles sell in the $8 to $15 range.

Puzzle values are often distorted when another type of collector is attracted by the theme on the puzzle, such as a Gunsmoke frame tray or a Mov-

Fig. 9-5 Die-cut, cardboard puzzles are one of the bright spots in the puzzle market.

Fig. 9-6 This puzzle (box shown in Fig. 9-5) contains 255 die-cut cardboard pieces.

ieland puzzle set with four movie stills from the 1930s. In the current market, the puzzle collector simply avoids the problem by not competing. In the late 1980s some aggressive collectors joined the puzzle collecting ranks. Some skirmishes have occurred, but there has been no major battle.

The most highly valued puzzles are mid-19th century examples and turn-of-the-century puzzles with strong lithographed pictures and box lids. McLoughlin remains a magic name among puzzle manufacturers, and their high value is directly related to the pricing philosophies that influence the game market. Many of these puzzles are designed for children, but in no way should the strength of these particular children's puzzles be interpreted to mean that all children's puzzles have value. There are almost no collectors of children's puzzles. Most collectors include a few examples in their collections, but that is the extent of the interest. Children's puzzles, especially those made after 1920, are inexpensive. They represent an excellent collecting opportunity.

One of the biggest misunderstandings in the current market is the degree to which one to three missing pieces affects the value of a puzzle. Dealers want to keep the discount to a minimum. Puzzle collectors feel it reduces value by 50 percent or more. The reason the values for puzzles with a few missing pieces remains high is that unknowledgeable collectors buy them. They are the hardest puzzle to resell.

Finally, dexterity and skill puzzles seem to be attracting a wider and wider audience. There is more competitive advertising in the toy periodicals for these puzzles than for jigsaw puzzles. Prices continue to remain low because collectors simply will not pay high prices. There is little reason to believe this will change.

PART II

CATEGORIES OF COLLECTIBLES

PART II

CATEGORIES OF COLLECTIBLES

CHAPTER 10

Toys

The individuals who experience the greatest joy in collecting are those who collect only what they like. Never forget this.

Ideally, every toy in your collection should tempt you to play with it. Yield to temptation occasionally. Toys were meant to be put into motion. Displayed on a shelf, they are in an unnatural state. Because of the age and cost of some (if not all) of the toys in your collection, you may feel the need to confine them to a display environment in order to protect your investment in them. This is understandable and, unfortunately, necessary. However, deep inside of you is the germ of a child. If not, you would not be collecting toys. Resist the urge to treat these childhood treasures as *objets d'art* and treat them first and foremost for what they are: toys.

There is no limit to the number of ways that toys are collected. Some collections are extremely broad, encompassing, for example, children's toys or vehicles; some are very narrow, such as one that focuses on Barclay civilian figures or Schoenhut Humpty Dumpty Circus material. Establish a collection philosophy that fits your pocketbook, space, and time available.

This chapter's purpose is to expose you to a wide range of toy collecting categories. Reading through them will help you make your first important decision: What toys do I want to collect?

Your decision is not going to be easy. If you are typical, you are going to be tempted by several categories. Remember, the scattershot approach is the least satisfactory method of collecting. It pays to focus from the beginning. Do not hesitate to change your mind along the way if your chosen category becomes dull and boring, although I hope this will not be the case.

If you have decided what to collect, or if you want to investigate more than one category while deciding, check all the available reference books that apply to the specialty. The list that follows is the most complete set of specific references ever compiled for toys on a category-by-category basis. General reference books were discussed in Part I of this guide; the books cited in this chapter are devoted to more specialized interests. These books are still in print or are readily available at libraries or through interlibrary loan. Early and/or obscure treatises are not noted here, but you can find them through the bibliographies in the books listed.

A few specific collecting hints are noted for each category. In no way is the information comprehensive. These hints are designed merely to stimulate your thinking.

Under each heading, where applicable, is also information on collectors' clubs and periodicals. More general collectors' clubs and periodicals were discussed in Part I, and no matter how much you specialize, you should always maintain a membership in one or more of these national organizations. Never forget your roots.

Read this chapter through from beginning to end the first time. After that, use it as a quick reference source.

Action Figures

Collecting Hints: "Action figures" refer to a class of plastic figures including items such as Hasbro's G.I. Joe, Ideal's Captain Action, and the Kenner Star Wars material. The figures have movable parts and a wealth of accessory equipment, ranging from costumes to vehicles.

Action figures arrived on the scene in the early 1960s. Because they are comparatively recent, tremendous emphasis is placed on condition and original packaging. Examples graded below C8 should be avoided if at all possible.

The category is very craze oriented, and speculation abounds. Both collectors and dealers tend to be on the young side. Action figures are not an area for the weak of heart or the conservative collector.

References: Carol Moody: *G.I. Joe Value Guide*, Hobby House Press, 1989. Steven H. Kimball: *Greenberg's Guide to Super Hero Toys, Volume 1*, Greenberg Publishing Co., 1988.

Periodicals: *Action Figure News & Review*, 39 N. Hillside La., Monroe, CT 06468.

Banks

Collecting Hints: Banks divide into two basic categories: mechanical (those with action) and still (those without action). Over the years, mechanical banks have proven to be a blue chip toy. In the 1980s prices for scarcer banks rose to astronomical levels, with many examples selling in the $100,000-plus range. New collectors are faced with two key problems: the high cost of entering

Fig. 10-1 J. & E. Stevens Co., Cromwell, CT, produced the Panorama Bank for Selchow & Righter Co. of New York City in the 1870s.

the field and the difficulty in telling some reproductions from the originals. Some of the older reproductions were extremely well done and now have more than 60 years of age behind them.

Still banks are collected primarily on the basis of the construction material, with toy collectors focusing primarily on lithographed tin and cast iron examples. Although less expensive than their mechanical counterparts, an average bank costs in the $75 to $200 range, which is steep for some beginning collectors. This area is also plagued by reproductions.

Both categories of banks are experiencing difficulty attracting new collectors, largely because most collectors under the age of 40 do not remember owning or playing with one. In addition, there is an "inner group" of collectors and dealers that only grudgingly opens its doors to admit new participants.

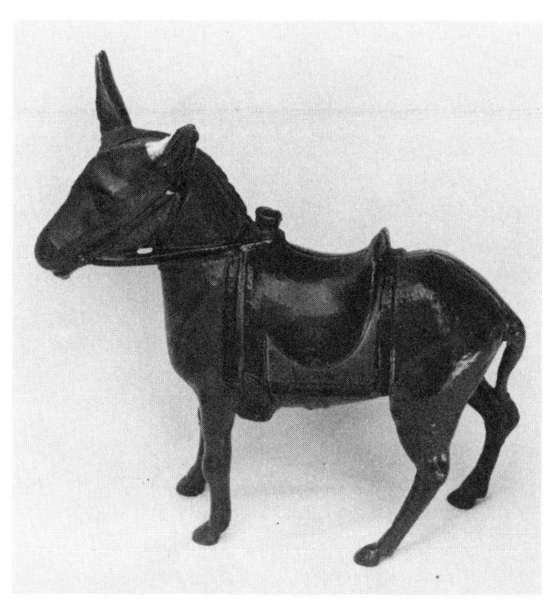

Fig. 10-2 Cast iron still banks, such as this Arcade standing mule, are a favorite among old-time still bank collectors.

Fig. 10-3 A specialized collection of "dime" still banks would number in the hundreds.

References: Don Cranmer: *Collectors Encyclopedia of Toys and Banks, Revised Edition*, L-W Books, 1988. Al Davidson: *A History of Antique Mechanical Toy Banks*, Longs Americana, 1987. Andy Moore and Sue Moore: *The Penny Bank Book: Collecting Still Banks*, Schiffer Publishing, Ltd., 1984. Bill Norman: *The Bank Book: The Encyclopedia of Mechanical Bank Collecting*, Accent Studios, 1984.

Collectors' Clubs: Mechanical Bank Collectors of America, P.O. Box 128, Allegan, MI 49010; Still Bank Collectors Club, 62 Hazelwood, Newark, OH 43055.

Battery-Operated Toys

Collecting Hints: It was the Japanese that introduced the battery-operated toy to the world market. Prior to World War II, U.S. and European toy manufacturers used batteries only to add realism to their toys, such as, allowing the lights on an automobile to operate. After World War II, the Japanese started using batteries to put toys in motion.

The golden age of battery-operated toys occurred between 1945 and the late 1960s. When collecting, seek lithographed tin examples rather than later plastic models. Packaging is critical, often adding 50 percent or more to the value.

Because battery-operated toys are action toys, they must be in working order to demand full price. The more actions the toy makes, the better (major action toys perform three or more feats). Corrosion in the battery case can seriously affect value.

American collectors compete with Japanese collectors for battery-operated toys. Many of the rarest examples quickly find their way overseas. Favorite forms are robots and space-related toys.

Because the average price for a battery-operated toy is about $200, they have attracted the interest of several of the New York auction houses. Prices

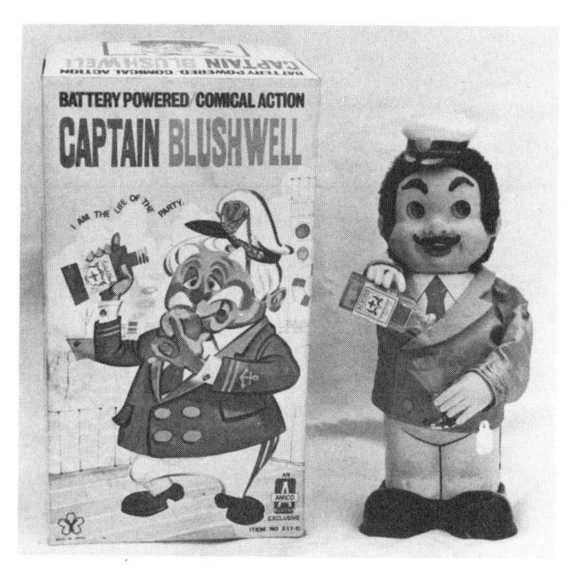

Fig. 10-4 Among the many aspects that attract collectors to battery-operated toys is their nonsensical character.

in the thousands are not uncommon for the scarcer examples.

References: Brian Moran: *Battery Toys: The Modern Automata*, Schiffer Publishing, Ltd., 1984.

Cast Iron Toys

Collecting Hints: Cast iron is a traditional category that has been broken up and assigned to other, more modern category designations. Today look for cast iron toys in the bank, farm toy, gun, toy soldier, and vehicle categories. There are still a few old-time collectors who concentrate on the broad spectrum of cast iron toys, but their number dwindles almost daily.

Cast iron collectors tend to focus on selected companies, such as Arcade or Hubley. There were hundreds of cast iron companies that produced toys, often as a secondary product. Some collectors concentrate only on minor manufacturers or manufacturers from a small geographic region.

The keys to collecting are originality and original paint. Many of the toys rusted; hence, they

Fig. 10-5 Arcade, who made this truck, was among the leading American cast iron toy manufacturers.

were repainted frequently. Loss of original paint can often lower a toy's value by 50 percent or more. Reproductions and copycats are numerous. Some dealers offer newly cast replacement parts, especially wheels. Before purchasing it, never fail to ask how much restoration work, if any, was performed on a toy.

Celluloid Toys

Collecting Hints: Celluloid toys have been neglected by most of the toy collecting community. Upscale collectors consider them cheap novelties. However, the increasing collectibility of holiday material, especially Christmas items, has resulted in a pricing level for celluloid that makes the category difficult to ignore.

It is still possible to find great examples in the $20 to $40 dollar range, due in part to the non-action characteristics of many of the examples. American collectors are also reacting to increased interest in celluloid toys from collectors in Europe and Japan, the manufacturing sources for many of the examples.

Celluloid is easily damaged through handling or heat. Do not buy cracked or damaged examples, no matter how low the price. Many items originally contained painted highlights that have been lost over the years, so beware of any celluloid toy that is only ivory or off-white. Loss of paint highlights decreases the value by 50 percent or more.

Fig. 10-6 Many celluloid toys were designed for young children.

References: Teruhisa Kitahara: *Yesterday's Toys, Volume 1: Celluloid Dolls, Clowns, and Animals*, Chronicle Books, 1988.

Character Toys

Collecting Hints: Pick one group of characters, such as cowboy heroes, or one character, such as Hopalong Cassidy, and concentrate on it. Toy collectors do not distinguish between fictional characters like the Lone Ranger and personalities like Gene Autry. You may wish to do so.

The character toy category includes every character and personality from comic books, comic strips, movies, stage, radio, and television. Popularity counts. The more popular a figure, the more likely material related to that figure will be collectible. The number of individuals collecting material on forgotten characters is small. Who remembers Little Annie Rooney? Is she from the comic pages, radio, stage, or screen?

Fig. 10-7 A Barney Google and Spark Plug Scooter Race lithographed tin toy, circa 1924.

The golden age of character collectibles dates from the late 1930s through the early 1960s, a rather long time span. It is not uncommon to find hundreds of items linked to a single character. Collectors should identify as quickly as possible the most common examples, as scarcity is a prime value consideration.

Fig. 10-8 Television character toys are especially popular among middle-age and younger collectors.

This is a good category in which to speculate with modern toys. Bargain bins at toy shops provide inexpensive long-range investments. Purchase those toys most likely to break or with the greatest number of parts. Focus on those toys correctly picturing the character or personality. Abstract representations will not hold their value in the long run.

References: Fred Grandinetti: *Popeye: The Collectibles*, Krause Publications, 1990. David Longest: *Character Toys and Collectibles, First Series*, Collector Books, 1984 (1987 value update) and *Second Series*, Collector Books, 1987.

Children's Toys (Preschool)

Collecting Hints: This category includes toys used by children from infancy through the age of 5 or 6. While some children remember playing with toys from this time period, the nostalgia factor seems to be centered more in the parent than the child. Women heavily dominate this field.

Children's toys is one of the least developed areas of toy collecting. The category received a massive shot in the arm in the 1970s when Fisher-Price toys became collectible. Collectors are already beginning to squirrel away toys from Creative Playthings, Ding Dong School, and Playskool.

Heavily overlooked are the handcrafted toys of revivalist and specialized craftspersons. If they find a home at all, it is most likely in a folk art collection. Some of the toys are one-of-a-kind love creations for the maker's own children. The collecting potential is wide open.

Children's toy dishes have been an established collectible since the 1930s. However, children's toy dishes collectors tend to associate themselves with glass collectors rather than toy collectors. When collecting toy dishes, toy collectors prefer them in sets in their original packaging. They tend not to buy single pieces.

References: Linda Baker: *Modern Toys: American Toys, 1930–1980*, Collector Books, 1985 (1988 value update). John J. Murray and Bruce R. Fox: *Fisher-Price, 1931–1963: A Historical, Rarity, Value Guide*, Books Americana, 1987. Doris Lechler: Children's Glass Dishes, China, and Furniture, Volume I, Collector Books, 1983, and *Volume II*, Collector Books, 1985. Doris Lechler: *English Toy China*, Antique Publications, 1989. Doris Lechler: *Toy Glass*, Antique Publications, 1989.

Fig. 10-9 Toy dish sets have dominated the children's toy collecting category for decades.

Children's Toys (Bicycles, Carts, Scooters)

Collecting Hints: This category includes children's wheeled toys, including carts and tricycles. Bicycles are not included. Five years ago, pedal cars were also part of this category. Now they are a separate category unto themselves.

Most advanced collectors focus on the wheeled toys of the period from 1870 to 1915. They look for vehicles retaining as much original decoration as possible. Prices in the thousands are not uncommon.

Vastly overlooked are children's wheeled vehicles from the 1920s through the 1960s. Some bicycle collectors have begun to focus on tricycles,

Fig. 10-10 A wagon featured in the S.A. Smith Mfg. Co. (Battleboro, VT) 1915 toy catalog.

now that prices for balloon tire bikes have risen into the hundreds of dollars. Two other possible collecting areas are scooters and homemade vehicles, for example, soap box and other racers.

Disneyana

Collecting Hints: Mention Disney and nostalgia kicks into high gear. Every individual has been touched by the Disney magic at some point in life. This is one of the toy categories that is most driven by the heart, not the mind.

Disney collecting has already been through several collecting crazes, each successful in raising the general pricing structure of the field. Much of the 1930s material and scarce material from the 1940s through the 1960s sells in the hundreds of dollars.

The key is to collect one or two key Disney characters or movies. Of course, the most popular material relates to Mickey Mouse and Donald Duck in the character area and Snow White and other early Disney animations in the movie area. Two areas that offer strong collecting potential are: the Disney movies of the 1950s through the 1970s, and material associated with Disney theme parks.

Remember that Disney is worldwide. American collectors tend to look down upon Disney material from abroad, with the possible exception of early

Fig. 10-11 Linemar's Mechanical Mickey Mouse The Unicyclist is an early Disney toy.

Fig. 10-12 Toys associated with The Mickey Mouse Club make an excellent specialized Disney collection.

English Disney items. This is an oversight. Canada appears to be a ripe market for merchandise, as does the European continent. However, foreign collectors are waking up to their Disney heritage and beginning to raid the American market. In 1990 Americans were still the principal Disney collectors. By 1995 that could change.

References: Bevis Hillier: *Walt Disney's Mickey Mouse Memorabilia*, Harry Abrams, 1986. Michael Stern: *Stern's Guide To Disney Collectibles*, Collector Books, 1989. Tom Tumbusch: *Tomart's illustrated Disneyana catalog and price guide, Volumes 1–3*, 1985, and *Volume 4*, 1987. Tom Tumbusch: *Tomart's illustrated Disneyana catalog and price guide, Condensed Edition*, Wallace-Homestead, 1989.

Periodicals: *The Mouse Club Newsletter*, 2056 Cirone Way, San Jose, CA 95124. *Storyboard Magazine for Disneyana Collectors*, 2512 Artesia Blvd., Redondo Beach, CA 90278.

Collectors' Club: National Fantasy Fan Club for Disneyana Collectors, P.O. Box 19212, Irvine, CA 92713.

Farm Toys

Collecting Hints: If you live on a farm or in the Midwest, you are familiar with farm toys and their popularity. Not true for the bulk of the dealers or collectors in New England, the Middle Atlantic states, the South, and the West. Good pickings in these areas.

Farm toys are collected two basic ways: by manufacturer and by type. Many individuals received their first farm toy when a parent purchased a new piece of farm equipment. The toy was a miniature of the equipment purchased. The extreme loyalty to equipment manufacturers shown by many farmers carries over to the type of farm toys they collect. This is a market that remains uniquely American.

Not all toys were distributed by equipment manufacturers. Many companies made toy farm vehicles for sale through department stores, catalogs, and five-and-dime stores. Most were made of cast metal; they were expected to last.

Farm toy collecting has become so sophisticated that it is now a specialty unto itself, with its own publications and shows. Collecting standards have risen considerably over the past five years. Greater

Fig. 10-13 Farm toy enthusiasts collect over a broad range, from miniature toys of actual farm equipment to any toy closely resembling equipment used on the farm.

emphasis is now placed on original paint and packaging.

The market has been inundated with new limited and special edition farm toys and reissues. Pricing is highly speculative. Too few have been resold to establish a reliable market. In some cases the number of special editions has reached the point where collectors have simply abandoned the concept of owning one example of every model made.

Because farm toy collecting is so heavily centered in the farm community, it is subject to the vagaries of the farm economy. Dealers tend to hold material in inventory rather than sell at a loss during hard times.

References: Raymond Crilley and Charles Burkholder: *International Directory of Model Farm Tractors*, Schiffer Publishing, Ltd., 1985. Dave Nolt: *Farm Toy Price Guide, 1988 Edition*, published by the author, 1988. Richard Sonnek: *Dick's Farm Toy Price Guide & Checklist: Tractors and Machinery, 1886–1990*, published by author, 1990.

Periodicals: *Miniature Tractor and Implement*, R.D. #1, Box 90, East Springfield, PA 16411. *The Toy Farmer*, R.R. #2, Box 5, LaMoure, ND 58458. *The Toy Tractor Times*, P.O. Box 156, Osage, IA 50461.

Collectors' Clubs: Ertl Replica Collectors' Club, Highways 136 and 10, Dyersville, IA 52040.

Guns

Collecting Hints: The traditional toy gun was the late 19th and early 20th century single-shot cap pistol. They were made by the same manufacturers who made banks and cast iron toys. Collecting keys include size, quality of design, workability, and scarcity. In the 1970s some original molds were found, and modern examples were struck. These reproductions are difficult to spot.

Collectors in the 1980s discovered the roll-fed cap pistols popular from the late 1940s through the mid-1960s. Although initially associated with the rise in cowboy collectibles, the cap pistol market soon developed a life of its own. Price escalated from $5 to $10 to $25 to $40 for the most common models. In the 1990s the market is emphasizing a quality product. If it is associated with a cowboy hero, it is a bonus.

Fig. 10-14 Above is a Stevens Echo from 1930, and below it a Stevens Comet from 1885. The older cap gun is worth approximately four times as much as its younger counterpart.

Collecting emphasis is now centered on pistol sets—units consisting of one or two pistols, holster(s), belt, and any additional accompanying material. If the set is related to a cowboy hero, the box is a must. Original packaging also enhances non-cowboy pistols as well.

Among the collecting areas that still offer potential are guns made of products other than cast metal, pop and cork guns, rifles, and water guns of all types. Forget space guns. They already are the darlings of space toy collectors.

Fig. 10-15 Space guns have gone out-of-sight in price.

References: Charles W. Best: *Cast Iron Toy Pistols, 1870–1940*, Rocky Mountain Arms & Antiques, 1973.

Collectors' Clubs: Toy Gun Purveyors, Box 243, Burke, VA 22015.

Marbles

Collecting Hints: Marbles are collected by two basic categories: hand-made and machine-made. Hand-made marbles usually command higher prices than machine-made glass, clay, or mineral marbles. There are a few exceptions, such as machine-made comic strip marbles. (Comic strip marbles are being reproduced. Beware.)

Some of the rare examples of hand-made marbles are Clambroth, Lutz, Indian Swirls, Peppermint Swirls, and Sulphides. Marble values are normally determined by their type, size, and condition. Usually, the larger the marble, the more valuable it is within each type.

A marble in mint condition is unmarred and in the best possible condition, with a clear surface. It may have surface abrasions from rubbing in its original package. A marble in good condition may have a few small surface dings, scratches, and slight surface cloudiness. However, the core must be easily seen. Any hand-made marble in less than good condition is considered junk by most collectors.

In the 1980s the price of hand-made marbles skyrocketed. As a result, collectors are paying much closer attention to machine-made marbles. Marbles that sold for a few cents a few years ago are now in the nickel and dime class. Marble sets, especially those still in their original packaging, are commanding a premium price.

References: Paul Bauman: *Collecting Antique Marbles, Second Edition*, Wallace-Homestead, 1991. Everett Grist: *Antique & Collectible Marbles, Revised Second Edition*, Collector Books, 1988. Mark E. Randall and Dennis Webb: *Greenberg's Guide to Marbles*, Greenberg Publishing Company, 1988.

Collectors' Clubs: Marble Collectors Club, P.O. Box 222, Trumbull, CT 06611.

Fig. 10-16 A swirl-type marble, with outside lines of yellow and white and a multicolor inner core.

Metal Toys

Collecting Hints: When collectors speak of metal, they generally mean lithographed tin. British collectors even use the term ''metal'' instead of ''lithographed tin'' in their toy literature. But because lithographed tin was not only sheet metal used to make toys, it will be discussed separately from other types of metal.

When the term ''metal toy'' does appear, it generally refers to toys made between 1880 and 1940. Rarely is it used to describe toys made after World War II. In this sense, there is a bit of snobbery attached to the term. Lithographed metal toys, e.g., battery-operated toys, remained popular after the war. In the purist's mind, since these toys did not match the quality of those produced by old-guard firms such as Lehmann, they are not worth considering.

References: Gordon Gardiner and Alistair Morris: *The Price Guide to Metal Toys*, Antique Collectors' Club, 1980 (1987 value update). Gordon Gardiner and Alistair Morris: *The Illustrated Encyclopedia of Metal Toys*, Harmony Books, 1984. Constance King: *Metal Toys & Automata*, Chartwell Books, 1989.

Fig. 10-17 Lehmann's ''Tut-Tut'' auto and driver traditionally has been classified by European collectors as a ''metal'' toy.

Model Kits

Collecting Hints: Until the 1980s the principal reason for buying a model kit was to build the model. Times have changed. Today, collectors eagerly seek unbuilt kits as well as well assembled examples. This collecting category is still defining itself, and a few points are worth noting.

Model car kits currently dominate the field. There are some collectors of military aircraft and ships. The historical and civilian airplane and ship model market still appears to be in the hands of the builders, rather than the collectors.

Rapidly rising in popularity are figure kits. Beatles figure kits now sell for more than $100. The monster collecting craze currently has these kits in the $40 to $100 range. Look for kits by firms such as Aurora, AMT, Hawk, Monogram, and Revell.

The current collecting market includes kits from the 1930s through the early 1970s. Because collectors now place so much emphasis on kits from the 1950s and 1960s, they command prices far in excess of the earlier kits. Focusing on kits from the 1930s and early 1940s offers an excellent way to build a quality collection for a fraction of the cost.

The three standard descriptions for model kits are MIB (mint in the box, with original wrapping still untouched), BWB (built, with original box), and BNB (built, but without the original box). Because most model builders are amateurs, the quality of the built model seriously affects price.

References: Paul A. Bender: *Model Car Promotional and Kit Guide, 1990*, Brasilia Press, 1990. John W. Burns: *The 1987–1988 Collectors*

Value Guide for Scale Model Plastic Kits, published by the author, 1988.

Periodicals: *Model Collectors Digest*, P.O. Box 8943, Waukegan, IL 60079. *Plastic Fanatic*, W.M.C.A., 19088 Santa Maria Ave., Castro Valley, CA 94546. *Plastic Figure Playset Collector*, P.O. Box 1355, LaCrosse, WI 54602.

Paper Toys

Collecting Hints: Do not limit the term ''paper toys'' to paper dolls and soldiers; these two groups are only part of the paper toy market. Among old-time collectors, the term is used to describe wooden toys to which lithographed paper designs have been attached, as well as describing toys made entirely out of paper.

The key to collecting wooden·toys with lithographed paper is the amount of paper and the strength of the surface color remaining. In addition, many of these toys were pull toys; the wheels must be original to achieve the highest price.

The category also includes paper toy soldiers and dolls. Collectors favor uncut examples over cut ones. Also collected as part of this category are die-cut cardboard stand-up figures that have lithographed paper attached. Again, complete sets are the principal focus. The original box also is critical.

References: Blair Whitton: *Paper Toys of the World*, Hobby House Press, 1986.

Pedal Cars

Collecting Hints: The late 1980s saw a pedal car collecting boom. In the mid-1980s a pedal car selling in excess of $1,000 was a rarity. By the late 1980s several cars exceeded $20,000. In 1990 a pedal car broke the $75,000 mark. The market has been fueled by a wealth of new information about pedal cars and an interest in the field by a number of wealthy individuals, many of whom are connected with antique and classic car collecting.

Unlike other areas of the toy market that place strong emphasis on originality, the pedal car market's strongest emphasis is on appearance. It is not uncommon to find a car that has been stripped down to its bare metal, rebuilt, and repainted commanding a record price. This has been an accepted practice in the car collecting community for many years.

The market appears to be very strong superficially. However, the number of collectors is unusually small. The departure of a few key collectors at the top would cause a sharp decline in the market. The market needs a stronger base and center, and although these areas do appear to be gaining in strength, they still have far to go.

Fig. 10-18 A group of pedal cars offered for sale at an outdoor show.

Because it is a relatively new market, it is still not known exactly how many pedal cars have actually survived. There is a strong possibility that the attention now being given to pedal cars will result in examples flooding the market. The final shaping of the market will take place in the early 1990s; the end results are still uncertain.

References: Julian Thomas: *5-in-1 Pedal Car Reference Guide, Volume 1*, Thomas Toys, Inc., 1987. Julian Thomas: *Mostly Postwar Pedal Car Reference Guide, Volume 2, 1935–1970*, Thomas Toys, Inc., 1987. Neil S. Wood (editor): *Evolution of the Pedal Car and Other Riding Toys, 1884–1970s*, L-W Book Sales, 1989.

Periodicals: *Wheel Goods Trader*, P.O. Box 435, Fraser, MI 48026.

Plastic Toys

Collecting Hints: Currently, the principal focus of plastic collectibles, is on plastic action figures and model kits. Collectors are largely neglecting other plastic toys. Part of this is prejudice—most collectors consider plastic toys junk. Lack of knowledge also plays a big role because there have been no books or articles to define the field, and collectors are uncomfortable blazing new collecting ground.

As a result, plastic toys are very affordable and easy to find. As in all collecting categories, the quality of products ranges from fine to atrocious. But there is no avoiding plastic toys; they sold in every toy store. An opportunity awaits the daring collector who will collect and promote the material while educating the market.

Premiums

Collecting Hints: The word "premiums" refers to the radio show, cereal, and other promotional items from the late 1930s through the early 1960s. Premiums issued later attract little interest from collectors. Premiums essentially were giveaway items, obtained when purchasing a product or by sending in proof of purchase.

Premium collecting dates to the early 1950s, and is one of the oldest toy collecting categories. It has proven to be heavily driven by nostalgia. The generation of collectors who remember the premiums from their youth is dying and the field is not experiencing an influx of new collectors, due in part to the high prices of some premiums. The 1990s are a critical period; the potential for

Fig. 10-19 Plastic toys from Cracker Jack make a fun specialized collection.

Fig. 10-20 The Jack Armstrong Pedometer from Wheaties was a popular premium in the 1930s.

decline appears much greater than the potential for growth, especially in the more common material.

As the number of premium collectors decreases, more and more emphasis is being placed on condition and original packaging. Many premiums contained more than one unit, but in the 1980s, dealers often split the units and sold the parts separately. Today's collectors are less tolerant of this practice. Further, since many of these premiums arrived through the mail, collectors are insisting on having the original mailing package in order to have a complete unit.

References: Tom Tumbusch: *Illustrated Radio Premium Catalog and Price Guide*, Tomart Publications, 1989.

Robots

Collecting Hints: Robots have already been through several collecting crazes. One occurred in the mid-1970s, driven largely by a group of American collectors who discovered the joys of battery-operated toys. Another occurred in the late 1980s, fueled by Japanese buyers who were acquiring the toys as part of their national toy manufacturing heritage. Today, the American collector is no longer the leading player in the field.

Collectors favor lithographed tin over plastic and action over non-action. When purchasing a robot, make certain it has all its parts. Attached accent parts, often of plastic, were common. They frequently are missing. Premium prices are paid for examples graded at C8 (excellent) or higher. Values decline quickly with lower grading.

The original box is extremely important. Most had wonderful graphics showing the toy in action. In many cases the box displayed only the name of the toy and the manufacturer. Never assume the grade of the toy is the grade of the box. Grade the two items separately.

References: Teruhisa Kitahara: *Tin Toy Dreams: Robots*, Chronicle Books, 1985. Teruhisa Kitahara: *Yesterday's Toys: Robots, Spaceships, and Monsters*, Chronicle Books, 1988.

Fig. 10-21 As this robot walks, his chest opens to reveal a rotating gun that shoots. It is marked "Made in Japan."

Toy Soldiers

Collecting Hints: Toy soldiers is not a category for little boys or girls. This is an adult battlefield. Collecting toy soldiers is one of the oldest forms of toy collecting; it has been practiced for centuries.

The principal method of collecting is by maker, with Britains holding the most honored place in the collecting community. Actually, there were hundreds of companies that made toy soldiers. One might assume that figures from smaller companies would be most desirable, but in truth, collectors focus on the major companies because they are knowledgeable about what was produced and because fairly high standards of production were maintained, especially among European manufacturers.

Fig. 10-22 All toy soldier collectors like to find their figures in boxed sets.

There are many classifications of toy soldiers: mass-produced, handcrafted, and blanks painted either by skilled or amateur painters. It is critical that any collector learn how to distinguish each of these groups and recognize the quality keys in each. Casting one's own lead soldiers was common from the 1920s through the 1950s in the United States and still continues today in Europe. Casting kits make an excellent specialized collection.

Soldiers were sold in sets and by single figures. Collectors must spend time learning which figures belong in which category. Sets often contained accessory pieces, which must be present for a set to be complete. Sets still in their original boxes and wrap command a premium.

Do not be confused by the term "soldier." This category also includes civilian figures as well. Civilian figures, unless they depict a special person, rarely command the same dollar value as do their military counterparts. Even in the 1990s they are affordable, with high quality available for a modest expenditure.

There are a number of dangerous trends in the toy soldier field: Damaged figures are being restored and repainted without informing the end buyer of what has been done. Figures are being enhanced with new decorations or accessories, or are being reshaped into poses not original to the

Fig. 10-23 This dime-store "soldier" is actually a well-known personality.

manufacturer. Finally, reproductions and copycats are rampant in the market.

References: Peter Johnson: *Toy Armies*, Forbes Museum, 1984. Henry Kurtz and Burtt Ehrlich: *The Art of the Toy Soldier*, Abbeville Press, 1987. Art Presslaff: *Hitler's Army of Toy Soldiers Featuring Elastolin, Lineol & Tipco, 1928–40: A Price Guide*, published by the author, 1987. Richard O'Brien: *Collecting Toy Soldiers: An Identification and Value Guide*, Books Americana, 1988. James Opie: *Britain's Toy Soldiers, 1893–1932*, Harper & Row, 1986. Don Pielin: *The American Dimestore Soldier Book*, published by the author, John Ruddle: *Collectors Guide to Britain's Model Soldiers*, Model and Allied Publications, 1980.

Periodicals: *Old Toy Soldier Newsletter*, 209 N. Lombard, Oak Park, IL 60302. *Toy Soldier Review*, 127 74th St., North Bergen, NJ 07047.

Collectors' Club: American Model Soldier Society, 1528 El Camino Real, San Carlos, CA 94070.

Tin Toys

Collecting Hints: The term "tin" refers primarily to lithographed tin toys, although painted tin was common during the 19th century. The category is divided into key collecting groups: early toys (mid-19th century through the 1870s), 1880s through 1915, 1920 through 1942, and 1946 to present. The missing dates represent war years when tin toys were not produced.

Which period of tin one collects depends largely on two factors: financial ability and childhood association. Early tin is very expensive. It also is one of the principal areas of speculation in today's toy market, fueled in part by the auction houses

Fig. 10-24 Unique Art's Li'l Abner Band is one of the classic tin toys from the 1920–1940 period.

and prestige toy dealers. Prices in the $50,000-plus range are not uncommon.

Lithographed tin toys from the 1920–42 and 1946–60 periods became popular among collectors in the 1980s. Toys by Chein and Marx became rallying points. It was quickly discovered that a great deal of this material survives. Except for rarer items, prices have stabilized, due in part to renewed emphasis on Japanese tin.

References: Jurgen and Marianne Cieslik: *Lehmann Toys: The History of E.P. Lehmann, 1881–1981*, New Cavendish Books, 1982. Nigel Mynheer, *Tin Toys: Phillips Collection Guides*, Dunestyle Publishing and Boxtree, Ltd., 1988. Peter Ottenheimer: *Toy Autos, 1890–1939: The Peter Ottenheimer Collection*, Harper & Row, 1984. Maxine A. Pinsky: *Greenberg's Guide to Marx Toys*, Greenberg Publishing Company, 1988 (Volume 1) and 1990 (Volume 2).

Video: David Pressland: *The Magic of the Tin Toy*, available in the United States through *Antique Toy World*.

Tin, Japanese

Collecting Hints: The Japanese are major players in four main toy categories: battery-operated toys, robots, Japanese tin, and windup toys. ''Japanese tin'' usually refers to friction (the vast majority) and battery-operated cars made by the Japanese from the late 1940s through the early 1960s. The models closely follow American car models.

Fig. 10-25 Chein is a tin toy manufacturer that is beginning to attract considerable collector attention.

Fig. 10-26 Japanese tin, whether cars or space vehicles, is one of the hottest commodities in the current toy market.

In the 1950s, American car manufacturers often changed model style every two to three years. It was an era of elaborate grills and fins. Today, these cars constitute the bulk of the American classic car movement. Devoted car collectors often want the small toys related to their big toys, and hence, they are helping drive this market.

An interesting pricing phenomenon in this area is the premium paid for larger models. While not true in all cases, models more than 15 inches in length appear to jump significantly in value from their 8- to 12-inch counterparts. Styling and detail are also critical pricing keys.

The current emphasis on cars has allowed a large number of other types of Japanese-made friction toys to slip through the cracks. The one exception might be airplanes, which have already attracted the attention of some collectors. However, there is a wealth of material still at affordable prices that is available to the new collector. Look toward the juvenile and nonsensical toys, such as friction animals.

References: Dale Kelley: *Collecting the Tin Toy Car, 1950–1970*, Schiffer Publishing, Ltd., 1984. Teruhisa Kitahara: *Tin Toy Dreams: Cars*, Chronicle Books, 1985.

Vehicles

Collecting Hints: Along with toy soldiers, vehicles have the oldest collecting history within the toy community. Cast iron and lithographed tin examples from the 19th and early 20th century are "blue chip" collectibles.

Vehicles are collected primarily by form: airplane, automobile, fire equipment, horse-drawn, motorcycle, racer, trolley, and truck. Within each form, collectors focus first by manufacturer, then by time period, and then by material used in manufacture. Because of the tremendous number of examples available, it is necessary to establish strict collecting parameters in order to maintain control of the collection.

The vehicle market is truly international. Many of the early vehicle toys were made outside the United States and enjoyed an extremely broad worldwide distribution. Exported toys were the same as those sold within their country of origin. Although the principal foreign market is Europe, the Japanese and other collectors worldwide have been attracted to this market by rapidly rising prices during the 1980s.

Collectors focus on vehicles that can be easily identified. Many lack any markings. When collectors are uncertain about a vehicle, even when it clearly is old, they tend to shy away from it. The adage that states, "The more that is known, the higher the value," applies here.

This is another toy sector that has been inundated with new limited edition reproductions, copycats, and fantasy items. Collectors must recognize the highly speculative nature of these prod-

Fig. 10-27 Automobiles are the most popular type of vehicle collectible.

Fig. 10-28 Among vehicle collectors are a group who specialize in horse-drawn vehicles.

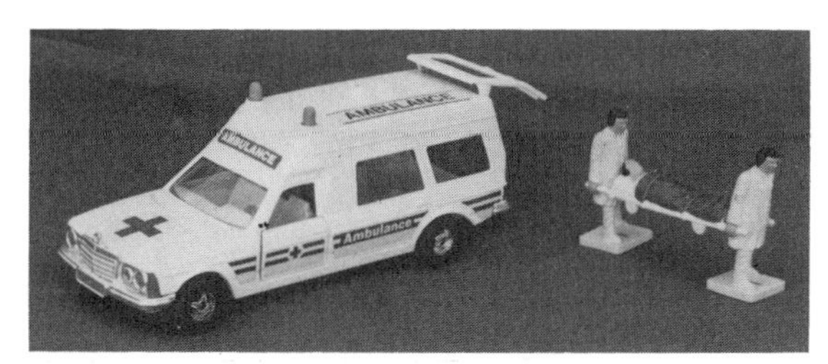

Fig. 10-29 Post-World War II companies, such as Corgi, already have a large block of devoted collectors.

ucts. Because they are being sold into a collection-conscious market, it is imperative that individuals who buy as a long-term investment never remove these items from their original packaging and store them under the optimum conditions.

References: Robert Carter and Eddy Rubinstein: *Yesterday's Yesteryears: Lesney 'Matchbox' Models*, Haynes Publishing Group, 1986. Edward Force: *Classic Miniature Vehicles Made in Germany, with Price Guide and Variations List*, Schiffer Publishing, Ltd., 1990. Edward Force: *Corgi Toys, with Price Guide and Variations List*, Schiffer Publishing, Ltd., 1984. Edward Force, *Dinky Toys, with Price Guide*, Schiffer Publishing, Ltd., 1988. Edward Force: *Matchbox and Lledo Toys: Price Guide and Variations List*, Schiffer Publishing, Ltd., 1988. Edward Force: *Miniature Emergency Vehicles*, Schiffer Publishing, Ltd., 1985. Cecil Gibson: *History of British Dinky Toys, 1934–1964*, Midansue and Modellers' World, 1966 (reprinted 1973). Lillian Gottschalk: *American Toy Cars & Trucks*, New Cavendish Books/Abbeville, 1985. Dale Kelley: *Collecting the Tin Toy Car, 1950–1970*, Schiffer Publishing, Ltd., 1984. Teruhisa Kitahara: *Tin Toy Dreams: Cars*, Chronicle Books, 1985. Teruhisa Kitahara: *Yesterday's Toys: Planes, Trains, Boats, and Cars*, Chronicle Books, 1989. Albert W. McCollough: *The Complete Book of Buddy "L" Toys: A Greenberg Guide*, Greenberg Publishing Company, 1982. Peter Ottenheimer: *Toy Autos, 1890–1939*, Harper & Row, 1984. Nancy Schiffer (compiler): *Matchbox Toys*, Schiffer Publishing, Ltd., 1983. James Wieland and Edward Force: *Tootsietoys: World's First Diecast Models*, Motorbooks International, 1980. Peter Viewmeister: *Micro Cars: A Collectors Guide to 3-in Miniatures*, published by the author, 1982.

Periodicals: *The American Toy Trucker*, 1143 46th St., Des Moines, IA 50311. *Automobile Miniature*, Rue de Saussure, 175017, Paris, France. *U.S. Toy Collector*, Box 4244, Missoula, MT 59806.

Collectors' Clubs: American-International Matchbox, 522 Chestnut St., Lynn, MA 01904. Matchbox Collectors Club, 141 W. Commercial Ave., Moonachie, NJ 07075. Miniature Truck Association, 3449 N. Randolph St., Arlington, VA 22207.

Wind-Up Toys

Collecting Hints: Toy manufacturers were using clockwork or wind-up mechanisms by the mid-19th century. They are still being used. Because the type spans such a long period, collectors usually focus their collecting on specific time periods. Traditionalists concentrate on pre-1915 toys, con-

Fig. 10-30 Action plays a large part when determining the value of a windup toy.

servatives collect examples made from 1920 to 1942, and more trendy collectors are concentrating on the post-World War II examples. Collecting by manufacturer is common. The golden names are Lehmann, Marx, Strauss, and Unique Art.

Because these are action toys, great emphasis is placed on their workability. Since the mechanism is hidden, its replacement with a new example is not seen as a major detriment. As with battery-operated toys, the more elaborate the action, the more valuable the toy is.

Surface design is also a major consideration. The vast majority of wind-up toys are lithographed tin. It is not uncommon for wind-up toys to consist of several independent parts, for example, Marx's ''Merrymakers'' mouse band. For a toy to achieve its full value potential, all the parts must be present. The original box is important, but does not seem to add the same level of value as do boxes in other categories, such as battery-operated or Japanese tin toys.

References: Teruhisa Kitahara: *Tin Toys Dreams: Wind-Ups*, Chronicle Books, 1985. Blair Whitton: *American Clockwork Toys, 1862–1900*, Schiffer Publishing, Ltd., 1981.

Wooden Toys

Collecting Hints: The use of wood as a toy medium can be traced back to antiquity. Construction sets, blocks, and carved figures (both static and action) are just a few of the toy forms made from wood.

This category contains toys made from wood with applied painted decoration, but wooden toys with applied lithographed paper designs are classified under the paper toy category. Wooden toys are divided into two basic groups: mass produced and handcrafted.

Mass produced wooden toys have not attracted strong collector interest, with the possible exception of the wooden toys of the 1943–45 era. During these war years the use of metals and rubber by the toy industry was highly restricted. American manufacturers had to make toys from wood and paper. One such example: those who grew up in the late 1940s and 1950s probably played with a ''Bill Ding'' construction men set. A wooden toy area that is attracting strong collector interest in the 1990s is the yoyo.

Handcrafted wooden toys tend to be classified as children's toys, since most of them are aimed at 2- to 6-year-olds. There are wooden toys for older children. Many evolved from basement workshop toys of the 1920s and 1930s. The home workshop was extremely popular, although most items produced probably were not toys. One collecting possibility is the kits issued by many manufacturers to be assembled in home workshops.

The problem with many toys is that they can be classified in more than one major collecting category. The principal category assignment can be found by consulting the general toy price guides, all of which are organized by category. While you may not agree with the category to which the toy is assigned, there is little sense arguing about it. The price guide classifications have become an industry standard.

CHAPTER 11

Games

When most collectors hear the word *game*, they immediately think of the boxed board game: a game that comes in a box containing a game board, an assortment of playing pieces, and instructions. Actually, the game category is much broader. Also included are adventure games (adult strategy games of the 1960s through the 1990s), card games, and skill games.

Games played an integral part of everyone's childhood. Therefore, it is only logical that when the collecting urge strikes, games are one of the first places many collectors turn. What gives vitality and viability to the game market is that most collectors collect the games of their youth. As each new generation of collectors enters the market, a new generation of collectibles is born. Game collecting will continue forever.

What makes game collecting more fun than most other types of collecting is that game collectors play with their games. Not only do they play with them, they involve their friends, children, and grandchildren. Games represent a bonding potential that is found in few other collectibles.

References: Lee Dennis: *Warman's Antique American Games, 1840–1940*, Warman Publishing Company, 1986.

Periodicals: *Name of the Game*, P.O. Box 721, Plainville, CT 06062.

Collectors Clubs: American Game Collectors Association, 4628 Barlow Dr., Bartlesville, OK 74006.

A Brief History

Games utilizing game boards date back to antiquity. A gaming board, playing figures, and dice were found in the tomb of Egyptian pharoah Tutankhamen. The Roman Emperor Claudius wrote a book about ''tabula,'' a game similar to backgammon, which the Roman legions carried across Europe and into Britain. Checkers is another game with roots in antiquity.

It is not uncommon to find the same games in many cultures. ''Chaturanga,'' a form of chess, was played in India as early as 600 A.D. It worked its way west via trade routes, assuming slightly different forms and names as it passed from country to country. One should therefore view games as evolving, rather than being invented. There are only a limited number of game types; there are thousands of variations of each.

By the end of the 17th century, a host of generic games were in place. In addition to backgammon, checkers, and chess were cribbage (based on an early game called ''niddy-noddy'', dominoes, fox and geese (a marble-jumping game), lotto, mah-

Fig. 11-1 Many early games were homemade, as is this version of nine men's morris.

jongg, nine men's morris (a version of tic-tac-toe), and parcheesi. In the early 18th century Edmond Hoyle, an Englishman, wrote a series of books focused on teaching the proper way to play the fashionable games of his era, one of which was whist, the forerunner of bridge.

Games played a part in the lives of American colonists. In New England, tenpins evolved from the banned game of ninepins; the Dutch in New York played skittle; Southerners found time for gambling and card playing. However, it was not until the industrialization of America in the first decade of the 19th century that games began to be mass produced and widely distributed, making them part of the average individual's everyday life.

The first mass-produced American games date from the 1840s. W. & S.B. Ives Company, stationers in Salem, MA, published several card games to supplement a line of stationery products. In 1843 the first American board game, *Mansion of Happiness*, was introduced, followed in 1850 by *Reward of Virtue*. Both games had strongly

Fig. 11-2 W. & S.B. Ives Company's Reward of Virtue. *Anne W. Abbott, daughter of a Massachusetts clergyman, designed the game.*

Fig. 11-3 Poetical Pot Pie *is one of the earliest known Milton Bradley games.*

moralistic overtones. By the mid-1840s, game manufacturing had spread across the country. William Langdon's *The Game of American Story and Glory* appeared in New Orleans in 1846.

By the middle of the 19th century, McLoughlin Brothers (1828), Milton Bradley (1860/61), and Selchow and Righter (1867 as Albert J. Swift, 1870 as Elisha G. Selchow) had entered the manufacturing picture. Parker Brothers followed in 1883. These four companies dominated the game market in the 19th and early 20th centuries. Following in their footsteps were hundreds of other manufacturers. Some, like J.H. Singer, had a national presence; others, like George A. Childs, were regional in scope.

Nineteenth century games are distinguished by the extremely high quality of the chromolithography on their box covers and game boards. As for playability, the amount of mental skill required was minimal, and the playing pieces also were rather plain.

Competition between game companies was fierce. To update a game, cover art was changed. Historical events quickly found their way into game form, such as Parker Brothers' *The Siege of Havana*. Many small companies only lasted a game or two. The situation continued until the end of World War I.

In 1920 Milton Bradley bought McLoughlin Brothers, and the big four became the big three. Actually, Selchow and Righter was always a weak

Fig. 11-4 McLoughlin Brothers' The Air Ship Game.

Fig. 11-5 To update a game, cover art was changed.

Fig. 11-6 George S. Parker & Company, publisher of Ye Peculiar Game of Ye Yankee Peddler, *eventually grew into Parker Brothers.*

Fig. 11-8 Parker Brothers' 1915 hit Pollyanna *remained in production for decades.*

sister in the market. It is more correct to write about the "big two." Each company strived to introduce games that would enjoy large popular success. Parker Brothers had a winner in its 1915 hit, *Pollyanna*; Milton Bradley kept pace with *Uncle Wiggley* in 1918.

In 1935 Parker Brothers introduced their version of *Monopoly*. Recent scholarship has traced the origin of the concept for the game to Lizzie J. Magie's 1904 *The Landlord's Game* and a host of similar generic games played in different sections of the country in the 1920s. Charles Darrow, who is credited as the inventor of *Monopoly*, actually patented a version of the generic game developed by Ruth Thorp Harvey and a group of players in Atlantic City. Parker Brothers' *Monopoly* went on to become the most successful board game in history. The company further strengthened its position by entering into a licensing agreement with Walt Disney.

In the 1920s the game industry discovered that

Fig. 11-7 Parker Brothers' The Siege of Havana *capitalized on a major historical event of its era.*

Fig. 11-9 Parker Brothers issued many different versions of Monopoly. *They have minimal interest to collectors.*

Fig. 11-10 Milton Bradley's Fibber McGee and the Wistful Vista Mystery *was a byproduct of a popular radio show of the 1930s.*

comics, movies, and radio programs were adaptable as board and card games. Games such as *The Game of Nebbs* and *Eddie Cantor and Tell It to the Judge* are among the many that were developed. Popular books, such as *The Wizard of Oz*, also inspired board games. In the area of generic games, Milton Bradley had hits with *Go to the Head of the Class* and *Sorry*.

New companies emerged. Among the more important are E.S. Lowe, J. Pressman & Co., Rosebud Art Co., Transogram, and Whitman (Western Publishing). But gone were the great chromolithography covers of the past. Although 1920s and 1930s box covers were flatter and often less detailed, they more than adequately represent the variety of illustration styles of the period. Die-cast gaming pieces appeared. During World War II, game companies stressed military theme games and old generic standbys.

In the 1950s the board game enjoyed a renaissance, due in part to the numerous games licensed by leading television programs. A host of new manufacturers such as Hasbro, Ideal, Lowell, Mattel, Remco, Standard Toycraft, and Whiting entered the picture. Milton Bradley, Parker Brothers, and Transogram continued as major players. Few television shows of the 1950s and early 1960s escaped having games created from them.

Fig. 11-11 Rosebud Art Company, publisher of Kitty Kat Cup Ball, *was a company that entered the game scene between World War I and World War II.*

The most recent major development in the game industry was the arrival of the adventure game, led by manufacturers such as Avalon Hill. These strategy games, designed primarily for adults, often last for days or weeks. The popular game of *Dungeons and Dragons* and its copycats is a juvenile market spinoff of the adult adventure game.

Game companies did not escape the corporate acquisitions and mergers that took place in the 1970s and 1980s. Milton Bradley became part of Hasbro Toys; Parker Brothers is a subsidiary of General Mills. New games seem to lack the pizzazz of past games. The number of character and personality-related games has dropped to the point where you can almost count them on two hands.

Fig. 11-12 Transogram's Tic-Tac Dough *is one of more than 30 board games devoted to the TV quiz shows of the 1950s and 1960s.*

The golden age of games that ran from the 1890s through the 1960s has passed, a victim of television and video games.

Boxed Board Games

Collectors of boxed board games can be divided by era into four distinct groups: mid-19th century through 1915; 1915–1940; 1940–1965; and post-1965. The title of Lee Dennis' book, *Warman's Antique American Games, 1840–1940*, is an excellent indicator of the prevailing attitudes among game collectors. Games made before 1940 have their interest; games made after 1940 do not. There is no question that this attitude is extremely short-sighted, but it is the prevailing attitude among the traditionalists.

Traditionalists control the American Game Collectors Association, so the main thrust of this group's meetings and publications is the pre-1940 games. The minority of members who concentrate on the post-1940 period are working to gain acceptance for their material. The recent publication of *Name of the Game* outside the auspices of the American Game Association is an indication that the post-1940 game collectors are a large group and seek an organization open to their interests.

If traditionalist game collectors had the choice, they would probably not buy a game made after 1915. Their fascination with the early material rests with the magnificent chromolithography on game boards and box covers. Although Milton Bradley and Parker Brothers issued games during this early period, the company that holds the hearts of collectors is McLoughlin Brothers.

In the late 1980s, there was a spectacular price increase in board games from the 1840 to 1915 period. The value of several top games went from the $800 to $1,000 range to the $5,000-plus range. The price gap between the top game and bottom game greatly increased. When the dust settled, the price for a McLoughlin game with average cover

Fig. 11-13 McLoughlin Brothers' Game of the Man In the Moon *was the first board game to break the $5,000 barrier at auction.*

Fig. 11-14 Clark & Sowdon's The Game of Golf *was produced with a spectacular chromolithographed cover.*

art was in the $200 to $300 range, with a large number of games in the $500-plus category. Even the most ordinary generic games of the period sell for about $50. One needs a deeper pocket now to collect board games from the earlier period.

This is not to say there are no opportunities in this category. The chromolithography of many secondary companies, such as Clark & Sowdon and J. H. Singer, compares favorably with that of McLoughlin Brothers. Their games are often discounted 20 to 30 percent because the companies are not as well known. Many collectors shy away from the most commonly found games. They try to find a game that no one else has or focus on "rare" examples. Common games, such as Peter Coddle games, are important social documents and should not be overlooked. Finally, restricting one's collection to only one type of game, such as comical conversation cards, also may allow entry at this chronological level.

Perhaps the most overlooked area of the game market is the period from 1915 through 1940. As pre-1915 material becomes more expensive and as more is learned about the games of the 1915–1940 period, more and more collectors are finding the 1915–1940 period to be fertile ground. The first wave of collectors is focusing on game box art, an approach that encourages price increases. Average games from the era sell in the $25 to $50 range, but this price level is under serious attack.

In the period from 1915 to 1940, games were far more responsive to larger events, making this an excellent period in which to develop theme collections, for example, automotive, electrical, or movie. Many playing pieces were die cast in shapes ranging from automobiles to radios. A collection of figural playing pieces may be ideal for a collector with a limited amount of space.

There were more game manufacturers during this period than at any other time in history. Many individuals developed games and marketed them regionally. Game manufacturers appeared on the West Coast. Collecting games on a regional basis is beginning to attract serious attention from several key game collectors.

The 1940 to 1965 period is the hottest part of the board game market, fueled by the collectibles market craze of the 1980s. Almost all these games are cross-collected, meaning there is at least one theme collector to compete with the game collector for every game. At the beginning of the 1980s a high price for a 1950s or 1960s game was $10. Now that number is approaching $100. The average game sells in the $25 to $40 range.

One of the characteristics of the post-World War II game is the large number of playing pieces,

Fig. 11-15 Four variations of Peter Coddle games: only a small sampling of the variations available.

Fig. 11-16 Whitman's Old Hogan's Goat *is typical of board game box art from the late 1930s.*

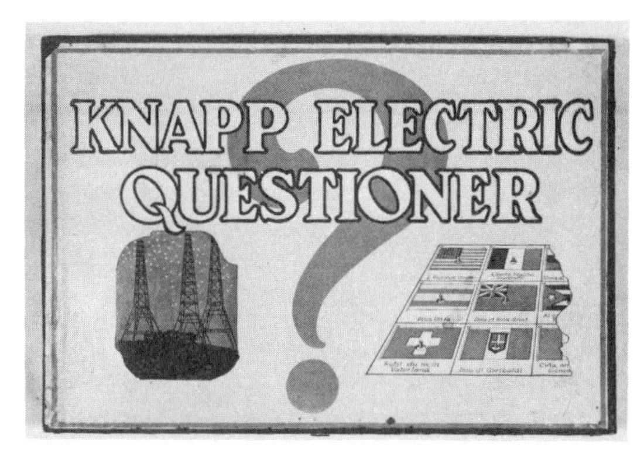

Fig. 11-18 The Knapp Electric Questioner *is just one of the many games that made use of batteries.*

Fig. 11-17 Wilder's Ocean to Ocean Flight Game *makes a great starting point for a collection of aviation games.*

ranging from play money to credit or penalty cards. Before purchasing any game, check the contents against the list found in the instructions. Subtract up to 25 percent of the price if up to 10 percent of the contents are not present; do not buy the game if the number exceeds 10 percent.

Board games from 1940 to 1960 are subject to collector crazes. As certain cowboy heroes gain and lose popularity, so does the value of their boxed board games. Since game collectors collect on a broad basis, they buy at the low point of cycles. In order to do this, they must follow their portion of the market much more closely than the pre-1940 collectors.

1970s games are in transition from a speculator-driven market to a more stable market subject to an occasional price run. Although many of the prices have stabilized, some, such as monster theme games, are in the midst of crazes. However, hoarding and speculation is much less a problem than it was five years ago.

Boxed board games from the late 1970s through the 1990s are being bought and hoarded by collectors and dealers in hopes of doubling and tripling their money in three to five years. This is pure speculation. Any purchaser is best advised to remember how many games were made and how many are in storage waiting to come on the market. Because so many of these games are being put

Fig. 11-19 Dexter Wayne's Ramar of the Jungle *illustrates both the nostalgic nature of 1950s board games and the growth of small regional game manufacturers.*

Fig. 11-20 Milton Bradley's Hopalong Cassidy Game *is typical of the growth of playing pieces in 1950s and later games.*

away new with the original plastic wrap unbroken, there will be new standards for the term "mint." Where has all the fun gone?

Adventure Games

Because of the fairly recent arrival of the adventure game on the game scene, the bulk of its collectors are within the player community. For this reason, the adventure game remains far outside the mainstream of game collecting. A number of individuals are moving past the playing aspect and beginning to assemble substantial collections—collections numbering 500 games and more.

Americans are in the forefront of all game collecting activities except adventure games. Although the adventure game has American roots, the greatest player/collectors are Japanese. They are willing to pay premium American market prices for an unopened game rather than take the time to reassemble all the pieces that become scattered when a game is played. Remember, some of these games can last for months.

The two principal ways of collecting adventure games are by manufacturer and theme. There currently are no catalog checklists to guide collectors, although it is widely believed that several are in preparation. Prices for the most commonly found games range from $25 to $40. There are many games priced in the low hundreds. Adventure game collectors have resisted the publication of price information about their games for fear of driving up the market and reducing their ability to find games below the market price paid by the serious collectors.

Card Games

Card games are often confused with playing cards. Collectors of playing cards, card decks with four suits of numbered and lettered cards, are not part of the traditional game collecting community. They have their own literature, collectors' clubs, and show circuit. For information about playing

Fig. 11-21 Adventure games were designed for adults, too, as seen by this Avalon Hill management game.

Fig. 11-22 The Cincinnati Game Company, successor to The Fireside Game Co., was an early card game manufacturer.

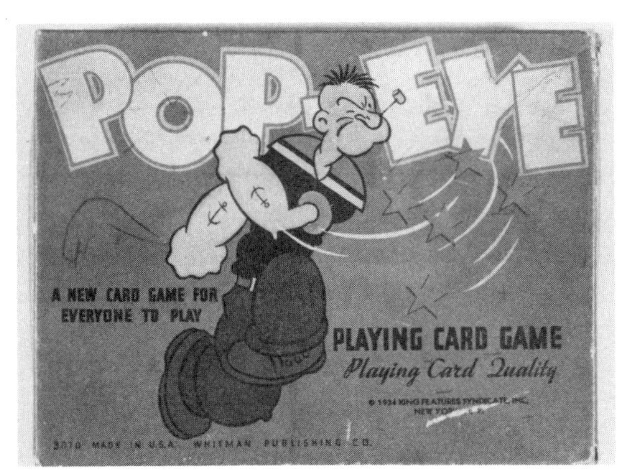

Fig. 11-23 Whitman Publishing Company has made a strong impact in the playing card game sector.

cards, consult the introduction to that category in *Warman's Americana & Collectibles*.

Card games that attract the interest of game collectors have an organizational basis other than the four standard playing card suits (clubs, diamonds, hearts, and spades). Old maid is an excellent example of a card game that appeals to the game collector. Card games have a history as rich as that of board games. By the last third of the nineteenth century, card games played a vital role in the game playing community. Many of the early games were educational, such as *Authors*.

This is one of the most overlooked segments of the game area. Many fine examples can be found in the $10 to $25 dollar range. Prices above $50 are rare, except for very early card games. When purchasing a card game, check first to make certain that you have the instructions (it is not always clear from the cards how the game is to be played) and then see that you have all the cards required. The cards' surface provides one of the strongest points of appeal for collectors.

Skill Games

Games using eye-hand coordination and played on a tabletop or on the floor, such as table croquet or tenpins, are skill games. Several involved a swinging device used to knock over stationary objects. Skill games went through several crazes, notably in the 1880s to 1890s, the late 1920s and early 1930s, and the 1970s.

This area of game collecting is largely ignored by most game collectors. The boxes that house most of the skill games are not appealing. The games are difficult to display and not especially showy when displayed. Many 19th century examples sell for less than $75. Examples from the 1920s and 1930s can be purchased in the $20 to $40 range, while 1970s skill games generally bring garage-sale prices of a few dollars, at most.

Fig. 11-24 Milton Bradley's Table Croquet *is typical of early skill games.*

Generic Games

There are a host of games that are not topical, not related to an historical event, character, or personality, and not associated with a cartoon, movie, radio, or television show. They are simply games that have survived in one form or another or one variation or another from generation to generation. Tiddledy winks and *Chutes and Ladders* are two examples. Few collect them. Yet, in many instances, hundreds of different examples are known.

For the collector fascinated with variation and its meaning over time, the generic game offers an ideal opportunity. It is the most affordable of all the game categories. Most examples cost between $5 and $15. A number of collectors have begun to carve out individual niches. However, because

Fig. 11-25 Wilder's Throwing The Bull *is a ring toss skill game.*

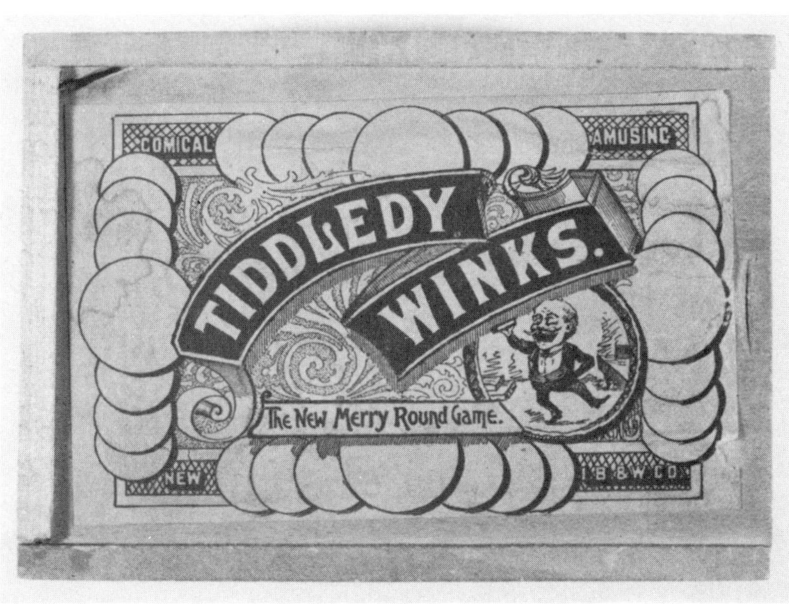

Fig. 11-26 One of the most famous generic games is Tiddledy Winks.

Fig. 11-27 One of the most overlooked collecting sectors in the board game area are games made for the American market by foreign manufacturers.

the number of examples is large and collectors minimal, the introduction of new collectors should have little to no effect on the market pricing structure.

In Summary

Game collectors are at the position toy collectors were 20 years ago. They are in the process of organizing and defining their collecting field. Only the most preliminary research has been done on the game companies and the amount of material available.

There are several established segments, but there are many unexplored areas that offer an opportunity to the collector who is looking for something both affordable and unusual. As the number of post-1940 game collectors increases, the traditionalist game collectors must open their ranks and incorporate this new group.

The major long-term question is how the field will handle modern video games when they reach the point of collectibility. Since the primary value of these games is their playability and not displayability, game collectors will have to develop an entirely new collecting mentality. It may not be possible.

CHAPTER 12

Puzzles

Normally, someone using the word *puzzle* is referring to a jigsaw puzzle. Although technically the name refers to puzzles cut on a jig saw, it has been broadened to include dissected, sliced, and water jet-cut puzzles as well. It is not necessary for pieces to interlock for a puzzle to be classified as a jigsaw puzzle. When assembled, jigsaw puzzles usually display a picture.

Actually, jigsaw puzzles are only one type of puzzle. There are many others, including put-together puzzles, interlocking solid puzzles, disentanglement puzzles, sequential movement puzzles, dexterity puzzles, and folding puzzles.

Jigsaw Puzzles

References: Anne D. Williams: *Jigsaw Puzzles: An Illustrated History and Price Guide*, Wallace-Homestead Book Company, 1990.

Collectors' Clubs: American Game Collectors Association, 4628 Barlow Dr., Bartlesville, OK 74006.

A Brief History

The origin of the jigsaw puzzle is open to debate. John Silsbury, a London map maker, is credited with producing the first dissected map jigsaw puzzles sometime in the early 1760s. Recent scholarship has revealed possible European examples prior to that date. Whatever the facts regarding the jigsaw puzzle's origin, it is safe to state that jigsaw puzzles were an accepted part of the toy market by the early 19th century.

The first jigsaw puzzles in America were English and European imports aimed primarily at children. Prior to the Civil War, several game manufacturers, including Samuel L. Hill, W. & S.B. Ives, and McLoughlin Brothers, included puzzle offerings as part of their product line. However, it was the period after the Civil War, especially the 1880s and 1890s, that saw the jigsaw puzzle gain a strong foothold among the children of America. In the late 1890s and first decade of the 20th century, puzzles designed specifically for adults appeared. Both forms have existed side by side ever since.

While jigsaw puzzles are usually associated with children rather than adults, it was adults who were responsible for the two major 20th century puzzle crazes in 1908–1909 and 1932–1933. The first craze focused on the wooden puzzle, so its societal impact was limited. But in the 1932–1933 craze the principal driving force was the die-cut cardboard puzzle, and its appeal was universal. The die-cut cardboard puzzle had evolved in the 1920s, and by the mid-1930s it was the principal jigsaw

Fig. 12-1 McLoughlin Brothers' Up The Heights of San Juan Hill *is typical of the children's puzzles commonly found at the end of the 19th century.*

Fig. 12-2 Movie Cut-ups were a popular die-cut, cardboard puzzle series issued during the weekly puzzle craze of 1932–33.

puzzle manufacturing technique. It made the jigsaw puzzle part of everyone's life.

The arrival of the die-cut cardboard puzzle did not end the manufacture of wooden puzzles. Among the large manufacturers, Parker Brothers continued making Pastime Picture Puzzles until the late 1950s, and Joseph K. Straus Products Corporation didn't stop cutting wooden puzzles until 1974. Skilled amateur cutters, semi-professional cutters, and small commercial firms—important suppliers of wooden jigsaw puzzles since 1900—have never ceased cutting jigsaw puzzles. Modern hand-cut examples tend to be expensive. However, a number of firms are experimenting with lasers and water jets, which may once again result in inexpensive wooden puzzles appearing on the market.

Interest in jigsaw puzzles has peaked and declined several times since the mid-1930s. One small revival occurred during World War II, and another was sparked in the mid-1960s when Springbok puzzles entered the American scene. At the moment, jigsaw puzzle sales are steady.

Fig. 12-3 White Eagle, *Movie Cut-ups No. 13, contains 300 die-cut cardboard pieces.*

Fig. 12-4 McLoughlin Brothers' Home Scroll Puzzle *shows the strong chromolithography on late 19th and early 20th century puzzles.*

Children's Puzzles

Collectors make a clear distinction between puzzles designed for children and those designed for adults. Although there are collectors of children's puzzles, the vast majority of children's puzzles are sold to theme collectors with interests in other categories. For example, an individual collecting television cowboy heroes is likely to pay more for a Gunsmoke frame tray puzzle than would a children's puzzle collector. Even children's puzzles from the late 19th century meet this fate: A McLoughlin Santa Claus puzzle set will likely attract more attention from a Santa Claus collector than a children's puzzle collector.

Traditional collectors clearly prefer children's puzzles of the pre-1915 period because of their strong chromolithography. Because the number of pieces is low and the cutting not very challenging, all the value rests in the surface image. Since the image was often duplicated on the box lid, the box is critical to value. Early children's puzzles focused on 4- to 12-year-olds, frequently combining education with entertainment.

Fig. 12-5 Milton Bradley's Playmates Puzzle Box *was aimed at younger children.*

Fig. 12-6 Saalfield's Just Kids *puzzle set was aimed at the 8-year-old and older age group.*

It is necessary to divide children's puzzles after 1920 into two groups: those designed for children between the ages of 2 and 7, and those designed for children ages 8 and up. Children's puzzles designed specifically for the younger age group have limited appeal unless they are early, as indicated previously, or contain art work by a famous illustrator. To date, collectors simply ignore them. One reason is the highly sentimental nature of much of the art work. Although not particularly plentiful, puzzles for young children made between 1920 and 1940 remain very inexpensive, presenting an opportunity to build a major collection for a minimal amount.

Until the mid-1920s teenagers and young adults were expected to content themselves with simpler adult puzzles. In the mid-1920s a number of major manufacturers, such as Milton Bradley, began offering die-cut cardboard puzzles with between 50 and 100 pieces. The complexity of the pictures

Fig. 12-7 This Our Gang *puzzle from a Milton Bradley Movie-Land set is typical of the 1920s die-cut cardboard puzzles that set the stage for the adult die-cut cardboard puzzles of the 1930s.*

and size of the pieces clearly identify these puzzles as targeting children 8 years old and older.

These juvenile puzzles tested the market for the die-cut cardboard jigsaw puzzle. Their success set the stage for the jigsaw puzzle craze of the 1930s. When the jigsaw puzzle craze hit, the juvenile puzzle was entrenched in second place while adult puzzles were king. Many of these early adult puzzles were movie related, meaning that the puzzle collector is in direct competition with the movie collector. Juvenile puzzles do exist, although now largely ignored by collectors. Disney theme puzzles and the Saalfield cartoon sets are the two major exceptions.

It was not until the early 1950s with the advent of the television era puzzles that children's puzzles received the attention they deserved. It was the juvenile puzzle, not the small child's puzzle, that dominated. Although existing before World War II as a form, the frame tray puzzle finally achieved a status equal to the box puzzle. Most of these puzzles are character and personality related, meaning that the puzzle collector must compete against a theme collector for almost every example.

Fig. 12-8 The frame tray puzzle offers an excellent opportunity to build a major collection for a modest investment.

Fig. 12-9 Milton Bradley's Mystery Jigsaw Puzzle: The Man From U.N.C.L.E.—The Impossible Escape *capitalized on a hit television series. It is a double purpose puzzle, combining a mystery story and jigsaw puzzle.*

Theme collectors have driven up prices to the point where most puzzle collectors, who are used to a much lower cost per unit, have shied away from them. This is a mistake. Many frame tray puzzles of this era still sell in the $10 to $25 range. Once again, specializing immediately is the key to building a good collection. One area of opportunity is frame trays relating to early TV cartoons and cowboy heroes. Ignore Hopalong Cassidy, Gene Autry, and Roy Rogers, however. Their frame trays are too expensive.

Adult Puzzles

When discussing adult puzzles, it is necessary to differentiate between those individuals driven by a collecting mentality and those individuals driven by a puzzle-making compulsion. Within the antiques and collectibles collecting community, most collectors focus on wooden puzzles made before 1940, although a few collectors now include some of the post-World War II Parker Brothers and Straus puzzles. A small number of collectors have discovered the die-cut cardboard puzzle. However, even their collecting emphasis is con-

Fig. 12-10 This adult puzzle combines non-interlocking cutting with cutting on the color lines. While it appears simple to do when viewed assembled, it is quite difficult when the pieces are separated.

centrated almost exclusively on pre-1945 examples.

Within the puzzling community, those individuals who derive pleasure solely from the act of doing the puzzle, there is a strong emphasis on the die-cut cardboard puzzles from the mid-1960s to the present. The reason is simple. They can be acquired cheaply at auctions, flea markets, and garage sales. Once they have been assembled, they are frequently given away, traded, or sold to get new stock for assembling. Within the contemporary puzzling community is a small nucleus of individuals who have begun to collect large blocks of puzzles from a single manufacturer. Provided they keep their collections intact, they will be viewed as pioneers 10 to 15 years from now.

Collectors and a small group of the traditionalist puzzlers are attracted to wooden puzzles for a variety of reasons. Many wooden puzzles, especially earlier examples, lack a picture key. They are viewed as more challenging. In addition, wooden puzzles are found in a large number of cutting variations. There are three basic types: interlocking, partially interlocking, and non-interlocking. Variation is added by the use of figural pieces, cutting on color lines, inclusion of false corners, open space in the center, non-rectangular borders, etc. Another feature of wooden puzzles is that the art work reflects the social tastes of the period when the puzzles are cut.

Collectors divide evenly among those who are fascinated with the puzzles cut in the period surrounding the 1908–1909 craze, those who focus on the 1920s cutters, and those interested in the puzzles made just before, during, and immediately after the 1932–1933 puzzle craze. It is for this reason that age often factors heavily into pricing considerations. Interest in post-1940 wooden puzzles is virtually nonexistent; this is a good entry level for a new collector of wooden puzzles.

By far the most important wooden jigsaw puzzle collecting criterion is cutting skill. There are basically six major classifications: large-scale commercial cutters, such as Milton Bradley and Parker Brothers; medium size and small commercial cutters, often surviving only for a few years; semi-commercial or part-time cutters; skilled amateurs; rank amateurs; and skilled cutters working at a high-quality, low-volume level, who sell almost exclusively to wealthy customers such as Par and Stave. Within the first four categories, the level of cutting skill varies over a wide range. While the definition of what constitutes quality cutting differs from collector to collector, two criteria seem to be the degree of difficulty in putting the puzzle together and the amount of space between pieces.

The publication of Anne Williams' *Jigsaw Puzzles: An Illustrated History and Price Guide* will significantly raise the level of sophistication among wooden puzzle collectors. The price gap

Fig. 12-11 Arthur G. Grinnell of New Bedford, MA, is typical of the small commercial cutter. He sold puzzles such as Christmas Eve *under the brand name of Superior Picture Puzzles.*

between a puzzle of high quality and one of low quality will increase significantly. At the moment, the gap is narrow. Many quality wooden puzzles sell in the $50 to $75 range. Smart collectors are buying as many as they can afford.

New in the area of adult puzzles is the growing interest in die-cut cardboard puzzles of the 1930s and 1940s. Because the number of examples is almost endless, it pays to specialize immediately. The area currently attracting the greatest interest is the weekly jigsaw puzzles of the 1932–1933 jigsaw puzzle craze. They are very affordable at $5 to $15, depending on the company and picture.

However, real opportunity awaits those collectors willing to focus on die-cut cardboard puzzle manufacturers of the 1930s and 1940s on a state or regional basis. The vast majority of these puzzles are selling for less than $5. As more and more examples are collected and studied, key companies, such as Regent Specialties of Rochester, NY, are being identified.

Fig. 12-12 Die-cut cardboard puzzles were made in tremendous quantities in the 1930s by national and local puzzle manufacturers. George P. Schilcher & Son, printers in Allentown, PA, became puzzle entrepreneurs with The Essel Picture Puzzle No. 6, Trout Creek.

A key cut-off point for the adult die-cut cardboard jigsaw puzzle collectors is the mid-1950s, when Tuco ended production of its thick, noninterlocking pieces in favor of the thin, interlocking pieces used by most of its competitors. Collectors are making a serious mistake in ignoring the adult puzzles of the mid-1950s through the early 1980s. As noted earlier, a few members of the puzzling community are pointing the way. These puzzles are inexpensive and plentiful. Where else can you build a collection for dimes and quarters?

Wood or Cardboard?

A primary division among puzzle collectors is the material used to manufacture the puzzle: wood or cardboard. Traditionalists favor the wooden puzzle and shun the cardboard puzzle. There is an implied assumption that wooden puzzles are somehow better than die-cut cardboard puzzles. This prejudice is enhanced by the unique nature of each wooden puzzle. Since they are cut by hand, no two wooden puzzles are exactly alike. When talking with wooden puzzle collectors, they take pride in pointing out how much harder it is to work a

Fig. 12-13 Tuco's Daring Death In A Jeep *was made from 3/16" wallboard pieces and typifies the die-cut cardboard puzzles issued during World War II.*

wooden puzzle than a contemporary cardboard counterpart.

Wooden puzzles have always been identified with the monied class. They were never inexpensive, nor are they today. Although selling in the 1920s for a penny a piece, a 500-piece puzzle was well outside the budget of the average middle income family. The most prestigious contemporary cutters now charge $1 a piece or more. Even a 200-piece puzzle represents a substantial investment, especially when you can buy a 500-piece wooden Parker Brothers Pastime Picture Puzzle from the 1920s for one-fourth the price.

There is no question that the feeling one gets doing a wooden puzzle differs significantly from that experienced doing a cardboard puzzle. The pieces have heft. There is a permanency about the puzzle. The Upson Company, manufacturers of Tuco puzzles, recognized this and offered puzzles made from 3⁄16-inch wallboard. Other cardboard manufacturers also tried to stiffen their pieces, either by using several layers of cardboard or by sandwiching wood between cardboard. They never succeeded in capturing the unique feel of the wooden puzzle.

The cardboard puzzle also suffers from the stigma of mass production. It is not a one-of-a-kind item. In some cases, production figures number well above a half a million for a single puzzle. As a result, it is not difficult to duplicate prized pieces in another collector's collection. This frustrates traditionalist collectors who like exclusivity.

As a result, the pre-1945 die-cut cardboard puzzle represents one of the best entry levels into jigsaw puzzle collection. The puzzles are affordable; most examples sell between $3 and $15. The large number of puzzles encourages specialization. Among the popular collecting categories are Depression-era weeklies, manufacturers, illustrators, and theme. The list of possibilities is endless. Competition for these puzzles is minimal. Remember, the bulk of the collectors are focusing on children's puzzles from the 1870s through World War I or on adult wooden puzzles. Finally, as more collectors are collecting die-cut cardboard puzzles, they are beginning to realize that many of these

Fig. 12-14 The Everett Piano sliced puzzle by Cincinnati's Henderson Archer Lithography Company is one of the earliest point-of-purchase advertising puzzles known.

puzzles more than match the assembly difficulty of their wooden counterparts.

Advertising Puzzles

A Brief History

The use of jigsaw puzzles as advertising premiums began in the 1880s and continues to the present. They are obtained either as a point-of-purchase premium (you receive your puzzle when you buy the product) or through the mail by sending in a coupon along with proof of purchase. The advertising puzzle's "golden era" occurred in 1932–1933, when hundreds of examples were manufactured.

Researchers do not agree on the origin of the advertising puzzle. In the 1880s the Rev. E.J. Clemens of Clayville, New York, manufactured wooden map puzzles, identified as "The Silent Teacher," the back of which contained either an advertisement for Sherwin Williams paints or White sewing machines or bicycles. The connection between Clemens and Sherwin Williams and White is not clear. Likewise, no evidence has been found that either Sherwin Williams or White used the puzzles as advertising premiums.

Sometime in the 1880s Peter G. Thomson, a Cincinnati lithographer and game manufacturer, printed a sliced advertising puzzle for The John Shilliot Company Mammouth Dry Good House in Cincinnati. There is little question that this puzzle was an advertising premium. In the 1890s, Cincinnati's Henderson Archer Lithography Company manufactured similar advertising puzzles. A valid claim can thus be made for Cincinnati as the birthplace of the first "true" advertising puzzle.

Early advertising jigsaw puzzles were distributed regionally. C.I. Hood & Company's "Rainy Day/Balloon" puzzle, issued in the 1890s, first demonstrated the national potential of the advertising jigsaw puzzle. A few companies followed

Fig. 12-15 C.I. Hood's Hood's Four-in-One Puzzle *is one of six different advertising jigsaw puzzles used by the C.I. Hood Company to promote its products.*

Fig. 12-16 When you purchased Essolube in 1933, you received this advertising puzzle illustrated by Dr. Seuss.

suit. The advertising jigsaw puzzle continued to enjoy limited acceptance during the first three decades of the 20th century. Things changed dramatically in the early 1930s, when the advertising jigsaw puzzle became part of the 1932–1933 jigsaw puzzle craze. In fact, there is reason to believe that the advertising jigsaw puzzle may have triggered the craze.

By the mid-1930s, the advertising jigsaw puzzle slipped back into a secondary role. Almost every year since, a few manufacturers have used a jigsaw puzzle as part of their advertising campaigns. Thus far, more than 100 advertising puzzles from the post-World War II era have been documented, and research has just begun.

"True" Advertising Puzzles

Only puzzles obtained through proof of purchase or at the point of purchase are ''true'' advertising puzzles. Puzzles obtained by other methods must be discounted. Likewise, puzzles whose pictures feature brand name products as part of the pictorial theme, but which were not distributed as premiums, fail to qualify. When there are gray areas, such as a souvenir puzzle of an ocean liner purchased on the ship during a voyage, apply the point-of-purchase logic and the fact that you must get the puzzle as a result of purchasing another product.

True advertising puzzles are categorized in two

Fig. 12-17 This advertising jigsaw puzzle from Eveready Flashlight included no product advertising on the puzzle itself.

Fig. 12-18 Curtiss Candy Company's advertising puzzle for Baby Ruth.

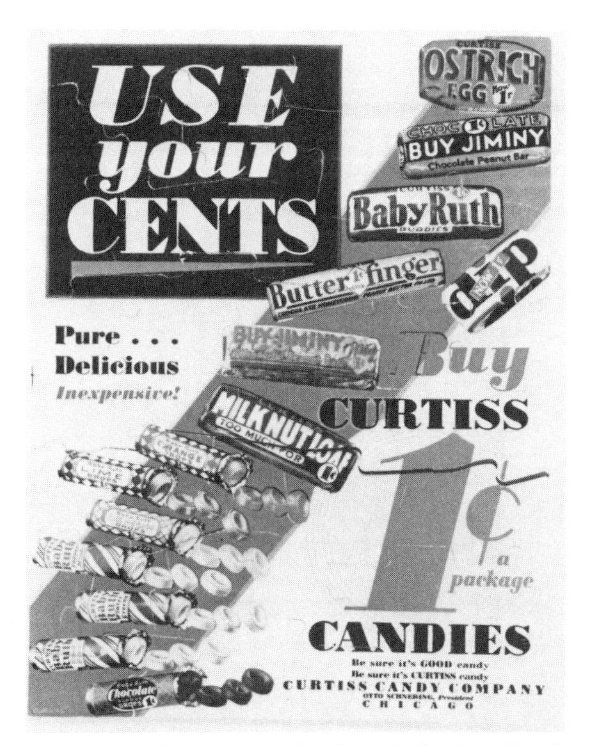

Fig. 12-19 The reverse side of the Baby Ruth Puzzle (Fig. 12-18) was an outright commercial for the company's candy line.

groups. The first consists of puzzles that do not feature the company's product on the puzzle surface. The puzzle theme is usually scenic. The advertisement is confined to the envelope and inserts. This group is further subdivided into: (a) puzzles manufactured specifically for one company and (b) stock puzzles used by more than one company or store.

The second category of puzzles features the company's product or products in the puzzle itself. Sometimes the reference is subtle, other times the puzzle is solely the company's product. This is the most desired class of advertising puzzles.

"Pseudo" Advertising Puzzles

During puzzle-cutting crazes, many private individuals cut jigsaw puzzles using an advertisement from a magazine or newspaper as the subject matter of the puzzle. These are one-of-a-kind advertising puzzles and are not considered advertising puzzles in the ''true'' sense when compared to their mass-produced premium counterparts.

Radio and Television Premium Puzzles

As with many 20th century collectibles, advertising puzzles are multifaceted. Several radio shows (primarily during the 1932–1933 advertising puzzle craze) offered jigsaw puzzles as giveaways. The puzzles focused either on the show, the advertiser, or a combination of both. A few television show advertising puzzles date from the 1950s. Although technically advertising puzzles, their principal classification remains ''media premium.''

Value

Advertising jigsaw puzzles are relatively inexpensive. Jigsaw puzzle collectors often ignore them. Advertising collectors are just beginning to recognize this important medium. Scenic puzzles in their original envelopes sell in the $5 to $12 range. Puzzles featuring personalities or scenes by famous illustrators fall in the $20 to $45 range. A top price for a premium puzzle is $75.

Double-Identity Puzzles

There are several cases where a jigsaw serves a double function. Among the more common examples are correspondence puzzles (a post card or letter cut into pieces and requiring assembly to read the message), mystery puzzles (read a short story and put a jigsaw puzzle together to obtain the clues to solve the crime), puzzles within a book (a not-uncommon practice in children's literature), holiday and seasonal greeting cards cut as puzzles, board games using jigsaw puzzle pieces, contest puzzles (name the puzzle or complete the limerick on the puzzle), crossword puzzles (assemble the jigsaw puzzle to get the answer to the crossword puzzle), and puzzle contest sets.

Fig. 12-20 Quaker Oats Company's Dick Daring *puzzle is more correctly classified as a radio premium puzzle rather than as an advertising puzzle.*

Fig. 12-21 This McLoughlin Brothers fire theme puzzle, which pictures the McLoughlin building in the background, is an example of late 19th century children's puzzles that rose in value significantly in the late 1980s.

Fig. 12-22 Look past the American border. Foreign jigsaw puzzles can be every bit as exciting as their American counterparts.

Only the mystery jigsaw puzzle and Little Golden Books with jigsaw puzzles inside their back covers have attracted strong attention among collectors. Most items in this category sell between $5 and $25, a very affordable price range for the collector wishing to specialize in the unusual.

For the truly esoteric collector, there is the category of edible jigsaw puzzles. The survival rate is not high. One begins by building a collection based primarily on contemporary examples.

Mechanical Puzzles

References: Carla van Splunteren and Tony Burrett: *Jerry Slocum and Jack Botermans Puzzles Old & New: How to Make and Solve Them*, University of Washington Press, 1987.

Slocum and Botermans define a mechanical puzzle as "a self-contained object, comprised of one or more parts, which involves a problem for one person to solve by manipulation using logic, reasoning, insight, luck, and/or dexterity." Sounds confusing. It is not.

Almost everyone remembers playing with a key-chain puzzle or sliding block puzzle at some point during childhood. Those who fancied themselves amateur magicians utilized disentanglement puzzles, often obtained from sets manufactured by A.C. Gilbert Company of New Haven, Connecticut. Even a child's architectural building block set qualifies as a puzzle.

Jerry Slocum and Jack Botermans have attempted to provide order to the vast mass of mechanical puzzles by creating 10 major classifications: put-together puzzles, take-apart puzzles, interlocking solid puzzles, disentanglement puzzles, sequential movement puzzles, puzzle vessels, dexterity puzzles, vanish puzzles, impossible object puzzles, and folding puzzles. Their book provides a detailed listing of the puzzles that belong under each heading.

Mechanical puzzles are one of the most underpriced segments of the puzzle market. A major collection can be assembled by spending less than $25 per puzzle, with an average cost in the $10 range. The key is to specialize. Some forms are expensive, such as puzzle vessels. A price premium is placed on age, thus making put-together puzzles from the 1930s worth two to three times the value of similar examples from the 1950s and 1960s.

Beware of buying any mechanical puzzle removed from its original packaging. Many types, such as disentanglement puzzles, were sold in sets. Some dealers split the sets apart for financial gain. Likewise, a review of the box art in Slocum and Botermans's book reveals a number of excellent examples of period promotional art. In some cases, the box art may be worth more than the puzzle enclosed.

In Summary

The jigsaw and mechanical puzzle market is an excellent place for the collector with a limited budget. There are a wealth of opportunities to assemble a major collection with a minimum of expense. The key is to define your approach and stick to it.

Some aspects of the category already have gone through their first significant price jump. The best example is the early children's puzzles from before 1915, which tagged along with the price run of games in the late 1980s. Wooden adult jigsaw puzzles and advertising jigsaw puzzles from the pre-1940 period appear to be on the verge of a price increase.

Above all, if you decide to collect jigsaw or mechanical puzzles, do so primarily for the joy of playing with them. This is their greatest asset. They can be used over and over again, often bringing the same degree of pleasure the 10th time as they did the first.

Fig. 12-23 Hollywood was a popular puzzle theme. This Susan Hayward puzzle contains 81 die-cut cardboard pieces.

CHAPTER 13

Ephemera

Once you become a serious toy, game, or puzzle collector, it is a natural evolution for your collecting horizons to expand beyond the actual objects themselves. As you research your acquisitions, you begin to realize there is a wealth of secondary ephemera that provides key information toward understanding the mercantile and cultural content of your toys, games, or puzzles. Ephemera breathes life into your toys, games, and puzzles.

At first, most collectors are reluctant to become involved in collecting ephemera because it means seeking material in non-traditional markets, primarily in the advertising, books, and paper sectors. Such fears are groundless. These markets are every bit as organized as the toy, game, and puzzle market. The same skills and techniques that you use to acquire the objects in your collection work equally well in acquiring ephemera.

The most limiting factor in collecting ephemera is too narrow a view. This chapter is meant to expand your horizons. The topics are by no means all-inclusive. Let your imagination run wild. Explore all the avenues that your research opens.

There is a fair amount of frustration in hunting ephemera, largely because few ephemera dealers have a clearly defined toy, game, and puzzle category. Seeking a specific issue of a magazine may require looking through thousands of examples. Ephemera hunting is time consuming. The key is having a well defined, specific want list that can be distributed to dealers. In addition, collecting ephemera is addictive. You can become so hooked that you devote more time to seeking the ephemera than you do the actual toys, games, or puzzles. You have been warned. Watch out!

Advertising

Advertising can be broken down into three major categories: broadsides, signs, and periodicals. Be concerned most about image and amount of information. Value is truly relative. Do not solicit or listen to outside advice. Except in very rare cases, the values quoted will have nothing to do with your interest. You and you alone are the sole judge of value in this material. So long as the object is priced below what you are willing to pay, buy it. If it is priced higher, forget it.

A poster is an example of a broadside. While broadsides and signs usually are one sided, collectors differentiate one from the other. Broadsides are printed on paper, while signs can be made from a variety of products, ranging from cardboard to lithographed tin. Both broadsides and signs played major roles in advertising toys, games, and

Fig. 13-1 Window broadsides such as this one were used to promote weekly puzzles during the jigsaw puzzle craze of 1932–1933.

puzzles, and were meant to have a relatively short life.

Although technically a broadside is a sign, most collectors view signs as an advertising item with more permanence. The key to any sign is the degree to which the product is portrayed. Collectors prefer pizzazz. A sign that is oddly shaped rather than rectangular attracts strong attention.

Essentially, there are three types of signs: product, manufacturer, and point-of-purchase, the latter often being a one-of-a-kind item. Product signs feature a product or group of products. Their lifetime usually was meant to extend through a selling season. Value increases when the sign is large, extremely colorful and vivid, the product has a strong central focus, and a recognized endorser is part of the picture. Manufacturers' signs tend to be logo-oriented and have an expected lifetime of several selling seasons. As such, they do not hold the same degree of attraction for dealers and collectors that product signs do.

Today, point-of-purchase material has begun to attract the attention of collectors. A few collectors began to save the large, two-dimensional cardboard figures used to advertise movies and videos. Cereal box collectors began placing emphasis on point-of-purchase cereal box displays. Recognizing a growing market, dealers have begun to advertise and seek out this material. Currently, the principal emphasis is on mass-produced point-of-purchase material. However, many point-of-purchase displays were done by a single store, either by their own promotion department or by a contracted service. Most of this material was destroyed. Collectors and dealers haunt department store and mall basements and warehouses in hopes of finding examples. Their efforts product spotty results.

Periodicals are included in this section primarily because of the advertising found on their pages and covers. Since the 1970s, it has become a common practice in the trade to cut magazines apart to sell single-page advertising. A surprising amount of advertising for toys, games, and puzzles can be found, but this pales when compared to the number of advertisements that feature toys, games, and puzzles in a secondary role.

The principal sources for this material are specialized paper dealers. To enhance the value of their material, they often mat it. In most cases, the cost of the mat far exceeds the cost of the matted item. When working with these specialized paper dealers, make it clear that you wish all items unmatted and at an unmatted price. Most collectors want the information for research, not display purposes. Do not spend money needlessly.

Catalogs

Catalogs are important research tools. They are the principal means for dating many toys, games, and puzzles. The vast majority of toys, games,

Fig. 13-2 The Carrom Game Board catalog from The Carrom Company, Ludington, Mich., is especially valuable because it includes rules of play as well as pictures of the company's products.

and puzzles manufactured before 1925 have no copyright or patent information. Finding the object pictured and/or described in the catalog provides a plausible working date. Remember, objects may appear in catalogs after production has ceased. Hence, a catalog date is a starting point for research, not an ending point.

Catalogs show the full spectrum of a manufacturer's production or a store's offerings. You can use the information from them to prepare a checklist of the objects needed to complete your collection. Manufacturers and stores issued both general and specialized catalogs, and you must carefully determine the nature of the catalog you possess. If the only catalog to survive from Parker Brothers was for their Pastime Puzzle line, for example, one would have a very distorted view of the company.

Catalogs can be used to document toys, games, and puzzles that were never produced. Many manufacturers used their catalogs as trial balloons for their products. Items were not produced until sufficient orders were received. Prototype toys, games, and puzzles occasionally do find their way into the collectors' market. Because their production was very limited, they are a prized item in any collector's collection.

Catalogs are classified into three groups: manufacturer, distributor, and store. Value is determined by age, number of illustrations, and number of pages. "Who made it?" is one of the most important research questions. For this reason, greater value is placed on manufacturers' catalogs than distributor or store catalogs. But do not discount the latter two groups; both can provide valuable information.

In the late 1980s the price of old catalogs skyrocketed. The price for an average catalog jumped from the $25 to $35 range to the $65 to $85 range. Toy catalogs priced at more than $100 are not uncommon. A number of institutions, such as the Margaret Woodbury Strong Museum, have begun to assemble research catalog files. Before spending large sums of money on catalogs, first check to see if you can obtain the same information from a research library. Since many of the catalogs are less than 50 pages, the cost to make a photocopy may be significantly lower than the cost to purchase the original. If you must own an original, then spend the money; if you only want the information, seek alternative sources.

One of the growing trends in the toy, game, and puzzle field is the catalog reprint. Some are done on a photocopy machine. Others are rephotographed and printed commercially. Prices tend to be on the high side because of the limited quantities printed. Check reprints to make certain there is enough information to make it of value. In a few cases, an expert or group of experts have priced the material illustrated in the catalog. This practice should be encouraged.

The vast majority of toys, games, and puzzles are sold during the last four months of the year. Large mail order houses and department stores issued fall/Christmas catalogs, which often contained very few toys, games, and puzzles. The reason is that most companies issued separate toy, game, and puzzle catalogs. These seasonal catalogs are important social chronicles. The type of toys offered says a great deal about prevailing attitudes.

Do not ignore the catalogs of the large five-and-dime, the neighborhood grocer, and the auto parts store. These were also important toy outlets during the holiday season. Distributors used stock catalogs. A store's imprint was added to the front and/or back cover when the store agreed to carry the toy line. The toys pictured in these catalogs are often not brand-name toys. Yet, they represent a far truer picture of the toy sector than does an F.A.O. Schwartz catalog.

Manufacturer's Materials

Catalogs, display material, and signs represent the most important manufacturers' artifacts available to the collector. However, if you focus on these items alone, you will miss a wealth of secondary material that can do much to round out a collection.

One obvious type of additional material is a manufacturer's letterhead, billhead, and envelopes. Manufacturers that produced toys, games, and puzzles over an extended period of time probably changed their letterhead style several times. Whenever a company changed its logo, new stationery was issued. Stationery products can be extremely helpful in dating a specific toy, game, or puzzle.

Fig. 13-3 A stock Christmas toy catalog from 1952–53.

Other manufacturer memorabilia that can prove helpful includes annual reports, memoranda and other inter-office communication, original product and design art, employee newsletters, and sales representatives' sample cases. Annual reports are available only for the larger, publicly held companies. Since many of the toy, game, and puzzle companies were small and privately held, formal annual reports may not exist. If you can determine the date of a company's annual meeting, check the local newspaper to see if a report was printed about the meeting. You may be surprised by what you find.

The toy, game, and puzzle business has always been secretive. Stealing ideas was quite common. Manufacturers guarded new product information until the product was announced to the trade at a toy show. Even when company correspondence does survive, there is extreme reluctance to make it accessible. However, collectors now recognize two key periods when such information does tend to become available: when one company acquires another, and when a company ceases operation. During either period, company records head for the scrap heap. A discreet inquiry can result in some first-rate material.

More and more recognition is being given to original product art, especially if the art is design development drawings. Few manufacturers recognize the value of this material. It is scrapped on a regular basis. It is not uncommon for employees to simply take it home when it was no longer needed. Original design drawings demand premium prices because of their one-of-a-kind nature. Today's manufacturers are more aware of the potential value of design drawings, and some are making a more conscious effort to save them.

Only a few toy, game, and puzzle manufacturers

Fig. 13-4 The American Nature Association used the jigsaw puzzle to promote interest in its activities through this advertisement in a 1930s Nature *magazine.*

issued employee newsletters. One example is the Upson Company of Lockport, NY, the manufacturer of Tuco jigsaw puzzles. The employee newsletter helps put the Upson Company's puzzle operation into proper perspective. One quickly realizes that the puzzle operation represented only a small part of Upson's production in the 1950s. The best source for employee newsletters is the area in which the plant was located. The most common means for uncovering them is an advertisement in the local newspaper.

Many toy, game, and puzzle manufacturers sold through a series of manufacturers' representative. In order for these sales people to operate effectively, the manufacturer had to provide a sales kit of its products. At the 1990 American Game Collectors Association annual meeting, a collector showed an album of box lid covers prepared for a McLoughlin sales representative. It was the highlight of the meeting. Next to manufacturers' catalogs, a sales representative's kit is the most highly prized piece of toy, game, and puzzle ephemera. Prices in the hundreds of dollars are not unusual for the few that become available.

Fig. 13-5 Theme magazine covers are eagerly sought by toy, game, and puzzle collectors.

Periodicals

Periodicals are divided into two types: industry and general. Industry related periodicals are extremely difficult to find in the ephemera market. Because of their value, there is a strong tendency among dealers who do find them to cut them apart and sell the pages separately. The only way to prevent this is to refuse to buy a destroyed copy. It is easy to resist the temptation when you remember that a photocopy of the same piece of information costs only a fraction of what the dealer is asking for the original page. When there are no more buyers for these cut-apart pages, the practice will stop.

When dealing with general periodicals, be alert in two areas: cover art and interior articles. The number of covers that picture toys, games, and puzzles is large. Often they are secondary, but they are there. Great value is placed on the cover art when it is by a famous illustrator or when it shows the play process. Covers that show the manufacturer of toys, games, and puzzles are rare, but do exist. Puzzle collectors are especially lucky, since the jigsaw puzzle theme lends itself so well to many artistic approaches. A collection of thematic covers makes an excellent secondary collection.

Toys, games, and puzzles went through crazes. General periodicals thrive on reporting the latest trends. Work with other collectors to make a list of magazine articles related to your special collecting interest. In many cases, you can pick up this material quite inexpensively, since most sellers focus solely on the cover art. If the cover is nondescript, the price is low. One such example is a December 1940 issue of *Life* which contains a marvelous story on the toys of the 1940 Christmas season.

Do not focus solely on American magazines. Toys, games, and puzzles are universal. Whenever you acquire a book about toys, games, or puzzles that was published abroad, check the footnotes and bibliographies for listings of foreign periodicals with toy, game, and puzzle covers and articles. Once you have a list, approach ephemera dealers in these countries and ask them to hunt for you.

Photographs

In the 1980s, collectors discovered another new source of information about toys, games, and puzzles: the photograph. The movement began with the doll and large children's vehicle collectors. Any picture of children with their toys or playing with their toys is eagerly purchased. It matters little if the photograph is a stereoscopic view or a black-and-white glossy by an amateur photographer. The key is that the photograph pictures an identifiable toy, game, or puzzle.

As collectors began to explore the photographic area in greater detail, they uncovered pictures of store interiors and store window decoration focusing on toys, games, and puzzles. Photographs of toy shops became desirable. A few smart collectors are approaching manufacturers for photographs of their display booths at toy shows, and approaching department stores for pictures of their Santa's playlands.

The price of toy, game, and puzzle theme photographs remains rather inexpensive, primarily because photography dealers have not yet established strong collector links with the toy, game, and puzzle community. Toy dealers are still testing the market. Good quality photographs can be found in the $10 to $25 range.

Do not forget to check with post card dealers. The post card format was used by many amateur photographs in the 1910s and 1920s. Although post card dealers charge a premium for these cards, the price is still affordable to the toy collector who wants the information contained in the card's image.

Beware of reprinted and rephotographed views being offered as originals. Individuals who are doing this often mat and frame them to make detection difficult. When viewing one collector's collection recently, I found that over half his photographic material was contemporary copies. I suspect his situation is not unique.

Fig. 13-6 The Upson Company proudly displays the products of its Tuco Work Shops in the window of the Lockport, NY, Chamber of Commerce.

Pieces and Parts

Many toys, games, and puzzles have greater value sold in their constituent parts, than they do when kept together. While most collectors and dealers deplore this trend, the truth is that it remains a major consideration.

Nowhere is this more evident than in the emphasis placed on the original box. The original packaging has assumed that status of an *objet d'art*. Now that we have reached the point where the original packaging can double, triple, or quadruple an item's value, it achieves a price identity unto itself. More and more, boxes without their contents are appearing on the market.

In some instances, such as in the case of early games and puzzles, it is not even necessary to have the entire box; the lid is enough. The elaborate chromolithography controls the value. The key seems to be the object's frameability. This also explains why game boards have attracted the attention of some collectors. Remember, when buying a framed item, you are paying a premium for the framing. When removed from the frame, the object often loses 75 percent of its value or more.

Other paper ephemera in toys, games, and puzzles includes instruction sheets, playing pieces, and manufacturers' promotional items, such as a miniature product catalog or announcement of the next product in the series. The removal of all this material from its original source must be discouraged. Simply refuse to buy it. Do not give into temptation.

Likewise, make a point to know what support material should be present in any toy, game, or puzzle that you buy. When it is not there, question the seller as to why. Look through his merchandise to make certain he is not trying to sell it independently. At a recent show, a seller offered a Cocomalt ''Flying Family'' puzzle with its original envelope for $45 dollars. Right next to it was a one-page broadside showing how one could become a Cocomalt Flight Commander, priced at $35. This broadside came with the puzzle. When I pointed out the separation to the seller, he readily admitted that he could get more money for the puzzle by selling the parts separately, and that few collectors were sophisticated enough to know that the two pieces belonged together. He was not going to change his policies; I plan never to buy from him again.

The amount of toy, game, and puzzle ephemera is unlimited. The principal purpose of this chapter is to introduce you to this fascinating aspect of collecting. I hope you will pursue some of these and other ephemera avenues as your collection grows.

What makes collecting ephemera such a grand adventure is that no one has the slightest idea of how much there is. Remember, most of the material in this category was designed for immediate use and then discarded. Every find has the potential to be a new discovery. Few toy collections contain truly rare items. Only the most wealthy can afford them when they are sold through regular market channels. Ephemera collections almost always contain several rare items, which is one of the reasons so many collectors get hooked on ephemera.

Because so much ephemera is two-dimensional, it can be copied easily. Learn to share. Pass along information to other collectors and dealers who have shared with you. In many cases, it is the information and not the exact piece that holds the greatest value. It is a quick, inexpensive way to establish a friendship in the toy, game, or puzzle sector.

Finally, there is ephemera to fit everyone's pocketbook, from inexpensive magazines to high-ticket original design art. No matter how much you have to spend, treasures await. Now it's time to go digging.

Author/Title Index

Subject Index

SUBJECT INDEX